DIM SUM STORIES

A Chinatown Childhood

GOLD MOUNTAIN STORIES

A series co-published by the Chinese Canadian Historical Society of British Columbia and the Initiative for Student Research and Teaching in Chinese Canadian Studies.

Series Editors: Jean Wilson and Henry Yu
Managing Editor: Jennifer L. Yip
Advisory Board: Jean Barman, Jennifer Chen, Victor Ho, David Lai, Chris Lee, Karin Lee, Colleen Leung, Peter Li, Imogene Lim, Patricia Roy, Jan Walls, Jean Wilson, Andrew Yang, Paul Yee, Henry Yu

Rebeca Lau, *Mami: My Grandmother's Journey*
Chad Reimer, *Chilliwack's Chinatowns: A History*
Larry Wong, *Dim Sum Stories: A Chinatown Childhood*

DIM SUM STORIES

A Chinatown Childhood

LARRY WONG

Chinese Canadian Historical Society of British Columbia
&
Initiative for Student Teaching and Research in Chinese Canadian Studies,
University of British Columbia

Vancouver, BC

This book is published by the Chinese Canadian Historical Society of British Columbia (CCHSBC) and the Initiative for Student Teaching and Research in Chinese Canadian Studies (INSTRCC) with permission of the author.

INSTRCC
University of British Columbia
http://www.instrcc.ubc.ca
   UBC's Initiative for Student Teaching and Research in Chinese Canadian studies (INSTRCC) has been built from the ground up by students collaborating with committed faculty and community groups. It focuses on recovering the rich and complex story of "Pacific Canada" as a geographical and historical concept.

CCHSBC
http://www.cchsbc.ca
   Founded in 2004, through its four-fold mandate of research, documentation, preservation and education, the Chinese Canadian Historical Society of British Columbia (CCHSBC) seeks to tell the history of the Chinese community in British Columbia.

Library and Archives Canada Cataloguing in Publication

Wong, Larry, 1938-
Dim sum stories : a Chinatown childhood / Larry Wong.

ISBN 978-0-9783420-7-4

1. Wong, Larry, 1938- --Childhood and youth. 2. Chinatown (Vancouver, B.C.)--Biography. 3. Chinese Canadians--British Columbia--Vancouver--Biography. I. Chinese Canadian Historical Society of British Columbia II. University of British Columbia. Initiative for Student Teaching and Research in Chinese Canadian Studies III. Title.

FC3847.26.W66A3 2011   971.1'3304092   C2011-903211-2

Cover photograph by Wayson Choy
Printed in Canada

I dedicate this book to the memory of my sister, Jennie (1931-2011). From her creative mind, she gave the world joy and laughter with her imaginary child, Binks, who was real to family and friends.

FOREWORD

Larry Wong has, I expect, been a storyteller all his life. In all of the years we have known each other, he has never been without a story to tell. Larry Wong was a founding director and then president of the Chinese Canadian Historical Society of British Columbia, his Chinatown play written for a local theatre is being encored, Larry's school tours of Vancouver's Chinatown have become the stuff of legend, his 'Ask Larry' website is a popular destination, and now he shares his Chinatown childhood with all of us.

Each of the stories from *Dim Sum Stories: A Chinatown Childhood* stands on its own and can be enjoyed separately, but together, just as with a dim sum meal, the end result is greater than any one of its parts. It is also the case, as with a dim sum meal that however much we relish the steamed buns, dumplings, and savouries, we save room for the dessert, and here too we are not disappointed.

Dessert at the end of a good meal gives time to pause and reflect, as Larry does in thinking back on his identity as Chinese, on the death of a mother he never knew, and on 'closing the circle' by going back to his father's home in China and to the first family left behind. Larry discovers they know far more about him and his life in Canada than the reverse. We glimpse the family dynamics that for virtually a century sustained men from China who came to North America at the cost of leaving parents and sometimes first wives back home.

It is relatively easy to write history from the outside, picking and choosing from among past times what appeals to us and then crafting events into a story we hope others will enjoy. To do the same from the inside, authentically and with feeling, is far more difficult, and this Larry Wong has achieved with *Dim Sum Stories: A Chinatown Childhood*. Larry is not afraid of honesty. We don't just visit Chinatown vicariously, we share with him the smells, the sights, the sounds, the everyday life of his childhood. We experience the inner workings of a Chinatown we only otherwise glimpse.

Larry's Chinatown childhood occurred in the 1950s, but it might as well have been much earlier in time. Chinese men had long left home in search of employment enabling them to support their families even as they made their way in a new land. In 1931, when Larry's oldest siblings were young, Vancouver's Chinatown contained 8,000 men in comparison to just over 200 women. Only a few men had been as enterprising as Larry's hardworking tailor father to get enough money together to bring over a second wife, even as he continued to support his first family in China. Larry's mother Lee Shee died when Larry, the youngest of six, was little more than an infant, and so his childhood reverted to the older ways of life that sustained the community. His acquaintances and minders were mostly the aging single men, to whom the young child must have given a glimmer of how different their lives might have been in other circumstances.

Larry Wong's Chinatown childhood is filled with the hope and joy of slowly changing times. The Second World War was a kind of catharsis for social relations. The Chinese men who fought alongside other Canadians and Americans were both emboldened and emboldened others that attitudes could and should change, and slowly they did so. Discriminatory anti-Chinese legislation was repealed and immigration once again became possible. Larry likely did not realize that when he made childhood friendships based not on skin colour but on mutual interests, by the time they all became adults, it would no longer be strange that they socialized on the basis of rough equality.

Indeed, as did many others of his generation Larry Wong worked hard to belong, becoming what he terms a 'Yellow Banana,' one colour on the outside, another on the inside. Larry did all the right things, attending the University of British Columbia and having a successful career with the federal government. It took him to middle age to re-find the Chinese identity he had given up as a young man in his determination to belong to a larger society that had for so long sought to exclude persons like himself.

We each see the past, as well as the present, through our particular sets of experiences. We remember vividly, and we also remember dimly. Larry's frank reflections give history immediacy and greater meaning. It is for these reasons *Dim Sum Stories: A Chinatown Childhood* is such an important book. We not only become a part of Larry's family and circle of boyhood friends, we also become a part of history.

Jean Barman

PREFACE

Some people may ask, "Why is there a Chinatown?"

I usually answer that there was a language barrier and plenty of racial prejudice. The Chinese formed their own community that became self-sustaining through family and benevolent associations. Most Chinatowns in North America were on undesirable land. In Vancouver, it was False Creek. Chinatown took shape on Carrall Street which ran into Gastown. Shanghai Alley was residential behind the businesses on Carrall. In 1884, there were 114 Chinese in Vancouver but this was deceiving. In fact, appropriately 15,000 were up the Fraser River and the interior building the Canadian Pacific railroad. In the 1950s, the Chinese population in Vancouver was 15,000. In the 1970s, it doubled. In the year 2001, there were 425,000 in Vancouver and the Lower Mainland.

When my Father first arrived in this country, he was greeted by young boys that shouted, "Chinky-chinky Chinaman!" It was a welcome he'd never forget. My father left a wife and a son, Wong Yung Tai, behind in China. It was an arranged marriage and the wife was expected to stay home to raise the family while my father came to Canada. In time, he sent for my mother from Kowloon. She came in 1921 on board the *Empress of Asia*. Father paid her head tax and married her at the old immigration building on Burrard Inlet. My mother died in 1940 and her remains shipped home on the same *Empress of Asia* that brought her here. Together they had six children. There was Git, my eldest brother who died in 1944 from an illness, Ching, my baby sister who died young, Wah, my oldest brother who died in 2001, Mee, a sister who died as a baby in China but was replaced with a paper sister, Jennie, my sister in Edmonton, and me. It is to them, I dedicate this book.

I also want to take this chance to thank Brandy Liên Worrall for her CCHSBC writing workshop that produced *Eating Stories: A Chinese Canadian & Aboriginal Potluck*. I learned a lot about writing from her. Many thanks, Brandy. Additionally, I want to thank Jean Barman for her friendship, and being my mentor, and Jean Wilson and Jennifer L. Yip, my editors for their patience and understanding. Without these four ladies, this book just wouldn't be possible.

Dim sum in Chinese means "a little bit of heart." In restaurants, it is a moveable feast of tasty little morsels of dumplings of various kinds such as minced beef, prawns, and pork. They come steamed, baked, or deep-fried. There are also steamed buns, sticky rice chicken, and even chicken feet for the adventurous. An infinite variety of choices. Textures range from the soft to the crunchy to the chewy. Tastes range from savoury to sweet. You pick and choose. It's a smorgasbord, all for your enjoyment and pleasure. Likewise here are not stories, but reminiscences of what it was like to live in mid-20th-century Chinatown in Vancouver. There are no story plots, no story lines; you pick and choose. Enjoy!

DIM SUM STORIES

Tea
jasmine, bolay, oolong

The family with Larry as a baby. Back (left to right): Wah, Father, Git
Front: Jennie, Mother, Larry

My Father

I was born in 1938 and, according to Father, one of the last babies delivered by a midwife in Chinatown. Within moments of delivery, she tried to cut the umbilical cord with a knife but the edge was dull. I was howling and crying as she shouted to Father for a rice bowl. He ran to the cupboard and grabbed the first bowl he saw and tossed it to her. She caught the bowl and grasped the wide brim; with the other hand, swiftly drew the blade back and forth against the bottom of a rice bowl. She stopped to feel the edge and wordlessly, slashed the cord, separating me from my mother.

Father heaved a sigh. He thought that for the five dollars a month he paid her, he was getting his money's worth. The payment was enough to look after my mother and included meals. Mother was forty years of age; too old to bear children in those days. I was the sixth and last child of my parents. My closest sibling was Jennie, seven years ahead of me. Father was born in 1891, the era of the Qing Dynasty. He grew up with the moral values from before the twentieth century. Mother on the other hand, was born in 1900 and as she grew up, the idea of a republican China appealed to her. She was truly a daughter of the new century.

My father's name was Wong Quon Ho but he used the public name Wong Mow as it was easier to pronounce and write in English. He arrived in Victoria, British Columbia, in May 1911 on a steamer called the *Chicago Maru*. He was twenty years old and had left a wife and young son back in the village of Lung Tow Wan, some sixty miles north of Macau. That same day, his $500 head tax to enter Canada was paid by compatriots from a benevolent association with the understanding that he would repay the loan. He went on to Vancouver, where he was offered a temporary place to stay until he could find permanent accommodations. He apprenticed with a tailor on East Hastings Street, not far from Chinatown, and easily acquired the skills of tailoring custom-made shirts. In time, he earned enough money to repay the $500 head tax owed to the benevolent association and, at the same time, send a small remittance monthly to First Wife and son.

My father's specialty was silk shirts. Lung Tow Wan was home to several textile factories and through people there, he was able to order silk directly. On advice from an experienced businessman, he brought in a partner to help start his business in Chinatown. Father took satisfaction in owning his own business, renting a shop on Main Street and attracting customers who sought him out. His customers weren't all Chinese; in fact, most were whites. The public market was across the street, as well as the old city hall, which later became part of the adjacent Carnegie Library, all of which had potential customers for him.

We lived between Hastings Street and Pender Street. Pender Street was Chinatown, and Hastings was where loggers, fishermen, and foreign sailors frequented hotel beer parlours, cafes, and pool halls hidden behind the newsstands. Few Chinese ventured to Hastings Street, and fewer Whites wandered into Chinatown. It was as if there was an invisible curtain between the two streets.

Streetcars ran past our store on shiny ribbons of steel rails. The Number 3 Main Street streetcar used to clatter and rumble and screech to a halt to pick up passengers in a designated area in the middle of the roadway at an intersection.

MY MOTHER

It wasn't until ten years later that my mother arrived from China. I never did find out how my father met her or how he arranged for her to be his second wife. It was obvious Father was affluent enough to take on a second wife and fetch her from Kowloon. All I know is that the General Register of Chinese Immigration shows that my mother, known as Lee Shee, arrived on board the Canadian Pacific steamer, the *Empress of Asia*, on January 31, 1921. Her actual name was Mark Oy Quon but she used the public name of Lee Shee for the same reasons that my father did.

Mother

The same record gave her age as 19 years and her height as five feet, one inch, and that she had both ears pierced. Her occupation was listed as housewife and her place of birth and home as Hong Kong. In reality, her home was Kowloon but the answer, Hong Kong, was easy enough to be understood by the immigration officers.

Unlike my father, she was held for questioning at the Immigration building down at the foot of Burrard Street, near the Canadian Pacific Steamship pier. Three weeks later, on February 24, she was released after her head tax of $500 was paid by Father, and in a quiet ceremony with one official and two witnesses looking on, she then married my father. When I was an adult, I looked up my parents' marriage certificate. It indicated that my mother spoke and understood some English. Their witnesses were friends who lived in Market Alley in Chinatown; my parents lived for a short time with friends in a house on East Pender Street, across from Lord Strathcona School, until they moved into the Loyal Hotel in Chinatown.

Mother was a beautiful woman. There is a portrait of her sitting in a rattan high chair against a studio background of painted trees. Her face is serene and delicate as she looks into the camera; she wears small dangling earrings and her dark hair is piled and swept back. Her right elbow rests on a pillar and her hands are joined on her lap. She is relaxed with her legs stretched out with ankles crossed and one heel resting on the floor. She wears a high-collared light-coloured silk jacket and a dark skirt. Both wrists are adorned with bracelets. Around her neck is a long necklace looped twice.

Father was happy making shirts for customers but I think Mother had a better idea. She suggested that he should also sell ties to go with the shirts and at the same time, sell socks and handkerchiefs too. Father did as she suggested and business improved. Then one day Mother thought Father should sell women's lingerie and women's hosiery as well. After all, she reasoned, customers had either wives or girlfriends, and what was a better place to buy such clothing than where their shirts were being made?

Most stories about Mother came from Jennie, my older sister. She remembered when I was a baby; neither bottled nor tinned baby food was available so Mother chewed my food before feeding me. She wheezed a great deal from a long bout of asthma. One day, she just couldn't breathe and had to go the hospital, but was turned away because there were no beds available. She went home and stayed in bed. Her condition worsened as she waited, and when I turned a year and a half, she died in her sleep. I never had a chance to know her.

Jennie also tells me how Mother played with us, taking great delight in laughing along with us. One day, Father said to me, "Your mother. She never called me by my given name. She always called me 'Wong' like 'Hey, Wong, what are you doing?' or 'Wong, let's go out and eat, I don't feel like cooking tonight.'"

My Siblings

The year after my parents moved from their friend's place and into the Loyal Hotel, Mother gave birth to Yung Git, my eldest brother. Father was obviously quite pleased. His second son! In the Chinese society of his day, my father's children born to a subsequent wife were also his First Wife's children, so for that reason my parents returned to Lung Tow Wan in 1923 to introduce baby Git to Huan Lu Lau and Father's first son, Yung Tai.

They stayed in the village for a short while before returning to Vancouver. The following year, they had their second child, Ching Won, a girl. Two years later, my brother, Yung Wah, was born. By that time, Father was ready to go into business with a partner; they formed the Modern Silk Company on Main Street, near Chinatown, in 1927.

The next year, in mid-summer, Ching Won became sick with tuberculosis and meningitis and died a painful death at the Vancouver General Hospital. She was three years old. In October of the same year, 1928, their fourth child, a baby girl was born and named Mee Won. The following year, my parents returned to China with Git, Wah, and Mee Won, but while they were in the village, Mee Won died. They were distraught, but with the help of First Wife, they found a family willing to sell a baby girl to them. She was approximately the same age as Mee Won and so also became Mee Won. First Wife agreed to raise the baby. My parents gave her Mee Won's birth certificate; in future, when the girl was old enough, she would come to Canada as a Canadian. She would become a "Paper Daughter."

My parent's fifth baby was Jennie. She was named Wong Jin Nee, avoiding the middle name of Won given to her older sisters. Jin is her middle name and Nee, her given. Her name in English is Jennie.

I was the sixth and last child. Mother was forty years old at the time. In my teen years I heard from friends that forty was very old for a woman to be a mother, and I often wondered whether I was conceived by accident or whether my parents really wanted another child.

Jennie, Wah, and Git on a farm in Ladner

MY HOME

My family lived in the back of the store. Our living arrangements were typical of Chinese immigrants, even in the mid-20th-century. We didn't have hot water, and Mother only used a small stone mill to grind rice and soybeans for homemade pastry, noodles, and bean curd. We used a wood burning stove and two small electric hotplates to boil water for making tea, washing, and cooking. The stove was also used to heat our living quarters during the winter. Our washbasin was deep enough to place enamelled pans for washing our faces in it. We had no refrigerator, but there was an icebox. A block of ice was either delivered to the store or my brothers would pull a small wagon a few streets to Hazelwood Ice Company on Keefer Street to bring one home.

A habit that has fallen out of practice nowadays is the art of haggling. When Father shopped at the nearby butcher shop for fresh meats and the fish market for seafood kept on ice, he could always talk a clerk into bringing down the price. He took great pleasure in his haggling skill: his grin would last until he came home with the groceries. We would eat vegetables such as bok choy, gai lan, choy sam, and watercress. These items came straight from the farmers to the stores in Chinatown. From the Chinese delicatessen we'd have roasted duck, chicken, and strips of barbecued pork. Sometimes we'd even have some roasted pig from the huge one that hung in their window. Then as now, there was no need for supermarkets if you lived in Chinatown.

EMPRESS OF ASIA

Across the street from our store was the Carnegie Library, built in 1902 from money donated by Andrew Carnegie, an American steel industrialist. The entrance was at the corner of Main and Hastings and inside a magnificent curved marbled stairway spiralled to the top floor. The library was impressive because of its two-story high stained glass window with the figures of William Shakespeare, John Milton, Edmund Burke, Walter Scott, Thomas Moore and Edmund Spencer staring at the front counter where books were checked out and in. On the third floor, after a dizzy climb up the spiral staircase, was the museum. I was fascinated by the collections of brightly coloured butterflies, the child mummy found in Egypt, and the tall costumed mannequin of poet Pauline Johnson in a display case, but the display that really captivated me was the model of the *Empress of Asia*. It was a Canadian Pacific Steamship built in 1913 that travelled between Vancouver, Yokohama, and Hong Kong. The model was easily over eight feet long.

As a young boy, I was drawn to the minute details of the miniature round windows, the funnels, and the riggings of the masts and even the lifeboats of the *Empress*. I used to sit on a nearby bench and gaze at this beauty, unable to take my eyes off her. In my imagination, I shrunk myself down to walk on the decks of the ship and enter rooms or galleries on board. I could easily hear the whistle blasting and the chugging sound of its turbines. I was spellbound, until I saw my reflection on the glass. I remember that while I was growing up, father kept talking about *"Ah Joe,"* and I couldn't understand why he and his friends kept talking about it. Eventually I realized that seemingly unrelated puzzle pieces throughout my childhood actually fit together. *Ah Joe* was Chinese for the *Empress of Asia*. I realised that besides her portrait, this ship was a link to Mother. This vessel carried Mother to her new land and returned her to Kowloon. The *Empress of Asia* was part of my family: my beginnings were here.

During and after the depression years, travel to China was possible but dangerous because of the Japanese invasion of China. Yet, my parents were compelled to return. They even opened a savings account with the Hong Kong and Shanghai Banking Corporation Limited in Hong Kong. However, the war between China and Japan hindered their plans until a year after I was born. I am not certain why they wanted to go. They were probably worried about First Wife, First Son, and young Mee Won. I suppose, too, that they wanted to introduce me to First Wife, but villages such as Lung Tow Wan were under attack from the Japanese Imperial Army. Communications were difficult as mail service was disrupted. The countryside was regularly bombed and there were many reports of looting, burning, killing, and raping of women. Villagers fled from their homes. Contact with Father's First Family was sporadic. Was it patriotism that made them to want to return to China? My mother was quite active in Chinatown by helping to sell war bonds to support the Chinese war against the Japanese.

Were they willing to take a risk of visiting heung hai, the village, in the face of the adversary? I have no answer.

Unfortunately, when they were ready to leave, mother was suffering from a complication of asthma and respiratory tuberculosis. She eventually took ill and died at home while waiting for a hospital bed. My father had no choice but to cash in the passage tickets and arrange for the shipment of Mother's remains to Kowloon, her village, for burial. Like most of her contemporaries, she didn't want to be buried in the hostile environment of Gold Mountain and preferred her home soil. She was to arrive home on the *Empress*.

Years later in 1990, I followed the notes that my siblings had written in a small black notebook about the precise location of Mother's resting place, but there was no cemetery. The locals told me it had succumbed to a building boom and all unclaimed remains had been ground into fertilizer. My moment of anticipation was shattered. I had wanted to see a physical marker of my mother. Instead a glass and concrete building stood in front of me. Had I travelled some 10,000 miles fifty years later only to be avoided by her ghost? I paused, listening to the din of the Hong Kong traffic, and asked myself, where do I place flowers, and where can I grieve in private? Like the fate of the *Empress of Asia*, which was sunk by a Japanese warplane near Singapore, her grave was desecrated and her remains lost forever. It seemed to me then, and still seems to me now, that my questions are without answers.

After Father's death in 1966, I feel as if I have inherited his memories and loneliness. I can still hear him sing himself to sleep with Chinese opera songs. At the time, I couldn't understand why he sang them, but I now know that they were duets he had sung with Mother. I can imagine the countless times he would reach across his bed for her only to feel the pain and loneliness of her absence. He would have turned his back, tears in his eyes.

HUMAN MEMORIES

Human memories are funny. When Mother died, I was told what happened, but I've never missed her or ever noticed her absence. I may have reacted to her absence as a baby by throwing a few tantrums and screaming my lungs out, but those baby memories are long gone. I was probably reassured that all was well. I probably called the women who looked after me "Mah-mah." The grownups assumed that I missed my mother, but to tell the truth, I really didn't miss her until I was an adult.

As I became older and realized I'd had a mother of whom I had no memories, Father would tell me bits and pieces of stories, but they may as well have been fairytales. There are a handful of photographs of Mother in the family album, and one of the few physical objects belonging to her, her wedding ring, my sister-in-

Larry at 20 months

law now wears. Sometimes Father would point to a portrait of Mother on the wall where there was handwritten Chinese calligraphy on the border praising her fundraising efforts and patriotism. And he would talk about the role of the *Ah Joe,* which had brought her here in joy and taken her back to China in tears. One day Father pulled from under his work bench a heavy wooden trunk and pulled open the lid, letting out the smell of camphorwood and mothballs. Inside, on a wooden tray, tied with a thin red ribbon, was a sheaf of long, flowing black hair. My father reached in and gingerly held it in his hands, "Your mother's," he said.

Mother's death was difficult for Father. He couldn't feed, diaper, or care for me in addition to looking after two sons and a daughter and run the shop at the same time. So my mother's best friend, Mrs. Anna Leong, took me in. She had a son and daughter who were older than me, but I fit into her family without difficulty. Shortly after that, I was transferred to Lillian Lee, who had three daughters, one the same age as me. Mrs. Lee's husband was a close friend of Father's so again I was quickly accepted into the family. When Father was ready to take me back, my sister, being all of ten years of age, played mother to me. Looking back on these memories now, I can see that Father was still grieving. My own grieving didn't really start until I was an adult when I fully understood the circumstances of my childhood and environment.

MY FATHER THE TAILOR

Father's customers were usually Caucasians or "lo fan" as we called them in Chinese. As a small boy, I watched them as they came into the shop and Father measured their neck, chest, back, and sleeve sizes. The customer had a choice of different colours from a wide selection of bolts of material such as crepe, cheviot wool, or gabardine. Once he had the measurements, Father used a pair of shears to cut a large piece of cloth from the bolt, outlined a template with chalk, and shaped the pieces. The sleeves, collar, and front button section were given special attention. Once the pieces were assembled at his Singer sewing machine, and the buttons were sewn, he moved to a button-hole machine for completion of the shirt. It was a very noisy machine, but it punctured the cloth material, stitched around the opening of the hole, and continued on to the next one. Father did this with the collar, the body, and sleeves, making certain the holes aligned with the buttons. Finally, he would iron the shirt and hang it on a hanger. Within three hours, he had a shirt fashioned, sewn, buttoned, ironed, and ready to wear.

Most of the time, his measurements were accurate and his customers were satisfied. All his shirts had double cuffs with three buttons, tapered collars, and double pockets with buttoned flaps; the tail was given extra length, which many of his tall customers appreciated. He guaranteed his workmanship. Some customers returned with a frayed collar, and Father would stop whatever he was doing. While the customer waited, he would remove the collar, reverse it and stitch it back on, all within minutes. No charge. Missing buttons? They were cheerfully supplied by Father. He was proud of his work and took care that his customers were happy.

At the end of the day, he used his abacus to total the day's sales. I was spellbound watching his dexterity as his fingers flicked the beads back and forth across the frame. In my teen years, I had to fill out a provincial tax form once a month, taking the sales figures from his school exercise book. He often tried to write his sales figures on a daily basis, though I've seen him pencil numbers from either from memory or imagination.

One of Father's most colourful customers was a rodeo rider who came early in the spring with a selection of silk materials. He admired father's style of shirt making. Father happily added the cowboy's requested white frills to the front, of the shirt and made a half dozen of the shirts. The cowboy rodeo rider proudly wore them at the Calgary Stampede. My sister told me that Father also made silks for racing jockeys. Some customers showed their gratitude for his workmanship in other ways, like the fisherman who tied up his boat at the foot of Keefer Street, where, at that time, False Creek came up under the old Georgia viaduct. He would come in after the fishing season and order several shirts. Not only did he pay in cash, but he also generously gave Father a carton full of canned salmon in mason jars which Father gratefully accepted.

Like most of his generation, Father wore his suit pants and vest with a shirt and tie. Whenever he had to step out, he'd slip on his suit jacket and his Stetson dress hat to look every inch the well-to-do businessman. Later in the summer, he made himself a little more comfortable by abandoning his suit, and wearing a trade mark shirt. The sleeves were three-quarter length, and the shirt had an open collar, and draped a few inches below his waist. It was grey in colour and he wore it only as working dress. I asked him once why it was grey and he answered that it hid the dirt well.

Father at his Singer sewing machine

Father always wore his hair in crewcut style, and in my early years I did, too. When he was in his sixties and seventies, it was difficult to believe he was that old because his style of haircut did not betray his age.

POP'S COOKING

One of the first things Father did in the morning was boil the water in a kettle on one of the hot plates and make tea. Our teapot was kept warm in a wicker basket and the tea, being steeped all day, was quite strong by the end of the afternoon. I remember hearing in the early morning the clip clop of the horse's hoofs on the cobblestone alleyway as the milk wagon ambled down the lane, stopping only when the driver delivered bottled milk to the back of our store. The delivery was actually at a cubby hole where the milkman picked up the empty bottles. In the winter it was so cold that the cream would rise out of the bottle looking like a neck with a paper lid on top.

On school days, Father made me breakfast, normally what we called "mush." It was actually Quaker oats and preparation took a long time unlike today's instant cereal. "Mush" was great during the winter, as it kept me warm while I trundled four blocks to school. Other times, Father made French toast, which was tastier than "mush." I suppose anything would be. Oddly enough, I still have Quaker Oats in the winter.

Father also made sandwiches for my lunch, a marked improvement over "mush." There were times, of course, when he ran out of ideas. Sometimes when I was home for lunch, Father would shut the store for a few minutes and walk to the On-On Restaurant on Keefer Street. There he would buy steamed bar-becued pork buns. Sometimes he bought the bigger buns, which contained pieces of chicken, onions, and boiled egg. Whatever he bought, the buns were always filling and satisfying. Other times, though, he would ask F.P., a family friend, to take me out.

One day, while coming home from school for lunch, F.P. met me at the corner and said that Father was too busy to make lunch. We walked to a café called Le Man on Keefer Street and sat down at the counter. A waiter wearing a starched white jacket and black slacks came over with a menu. F.P. said, "We don't need the menu. Two veal cutlets, please." The waiter nodded and placed knives, forks and spoons in front of us. Now, at home, we ate with chopsticks. Occasionally we'd use a fork to jab at a piece of meat or vegetables or something too slippery for our chopsticks. F.P. knew this and gave me a lesson on how to use a knife and fork. It seemed he worked as a houseboy when he first came to Canada and quickly learned lo fan etiquette. I was a quick student and from that day on, I became fond of veal cutlets, and especially loved wiener schnitzel.

Dinnertime, however, was something else. Father had only two hotplates and the wood burning stove in the kitchen, but he created wonderful meals. He didn't have a wok so he used other cooking utensils. In a Dutch oven he could roast a small chicken, drop a live fresh crab into boiling water, concoct delicious soup, and make stew. In the stew, instead of potatoes, he substituted Chinese radish or regular dried peanuts. Father also used a steamer for chicken, fish, like sturgeon or halibut, an egg custard dish, and my favourite, a tasty pork pie. He also had a frying pan, but it wasn't used much.

I remember well the rhythmic sound of his cleaver mincing a pork steak on a wooden block cut from a tree trunk. There was a rhythm to his chopping that assured a good meal. Father would add thinly sliced preserved turnips, sliced Chinese sausages, or even smaller pieces of salted fish before placing the dish in the steamer. My favourite dish was pickled Swiss chard with sliced beef. This was the Chinese version of sauerkraut. The pickled vegetable was always available in a barrel in Chinatown and it was always in much demand. It was savoury with a bit of vinegary taste, and not as strong as sauerkraut.

HOME COOKING

Occasionally I would go with Pop to the poultry shop and help select a chicken from a coop either on the sidewalk or inside the shop. The clerk would take the protesting bird to the back, and within minutes return with it dressed. Father loved cooking chicken, especially if we had company. There were so many ways of cooking it; you could boil, roast, steam, and fry it in an infinite number of ways. I believe there must be over a hundred ways to cook chicken.

Father also enjoyed cooking fish. One reason was that the fish market was just around the corner from us and so there was always a wide selection of seafood. There were sturgeon, halibut, rock cod, black cod, smelts, and salmon. There were plenty of fish then. Most of the time, Father steamed the fish to keep the flavour and texture, and, of course, there was crab. He would drop the poor creature into the boiling water until it turned red. Sometimes I swore I could hear it screaming, but that's all forgotten when one eats crab covered with black bean sauce.

Once I was trying to help Father in the kitchen by stirring a pot of soup with one chopstick when all of a sudden he boomed out, "Never use one chopstick by itself, use them in pairs." I gave him a dumb look. "It's bad luck," he said. "Always use them together." And that was the end of the matter.

DINNERTIME

In our living quarters we had a table covered with a red vinyl tablecloth that we used to read, study, and eat. When it was time for dinner, Father or Jennie would spread out newspapers over the table. Father would place the serving dishes, the rice bowls, and chopsticks on it and we would all sit down to eat. Occasionally there'd be beef bone from the soup, or bones from a fish or excess fat from a piece of pork: they went onto the newspapers.

As we neared the end of a meal, Father would exhort us to eat every single grain of rice from our bowl, and to make certain we left the serving plates empty, "Otherwise," he said, "We'll send the leftovers of our dinner to Hong Kong." Hong Kong in the early fifties was overrun with refugees escaping from the Communist takeover of China, and they were literally homeless and starving. Father felt so fortunate to be in Canada and did not envy being in Hong Kong. At the end of dinner, Father would clear the dishes and roll up the newspapers so as to wrap up the waste to burn in the stove. It was a very practical idea.

Jennie, always a voracious reader, read newspapers while eating. She was always careful to place the comics section in front of her. One day the paper was upside down in front of her: that was when she began to learn to read that way. To this day, she can still read upside down, displaying a hidden talent for which I can only roll my eyes heavenward and pray it continues to be kept hidden.

DINING OUT

There were times when Father ran out of ideas for cooking dinner and would take us out. There were lots of restaurants and cafes in Chinatown and so we had good selections. One restaurant I remember served western style food. Father ordered ox tongue. At first I made a face but when the food arrived and I tried it, I was pleasantly surprised at the texture. The meat came with mashed potatoes and a mixture of peas and carrots. I later found out that ox tongue was cheap meat, but unknown to everyone then, it had a lot of food value.

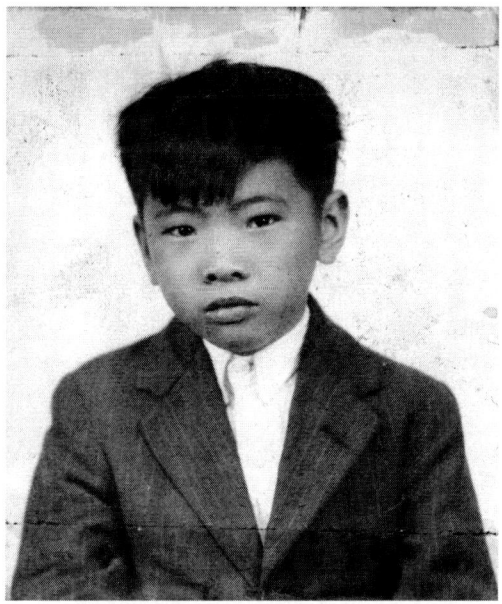

Larry's passport photo

Siu Yeh

I think siu yeh is the favourite eating activity for Chinese people. Chinese love their food. My father was no exception. After my siblings left home, I noticed that Father would come home late, sometimes two in morning. This was odd as I knew his friend, George Lee, closed his confectionery store at midnight. After a few nights, I either ignored or slept through his coming home late. Until one night.

I was sleeping soundly when I heard Father calling my name. I roused myself and with blurry eyes, peered through the darkness and saw a plate in front of me. The smell was of chow mein, and my eyes opened wide. Father pushed the plate of hot chow mein to my face and said one word. Eat.

Not being fully awake, I obediently ate the offering; as I recall, I finished the noodles and promptly fell asleep. The next morning, I had my usual breakfast of mush and went to school. I had forgotten about the noodle snack. Then two nights later, Father woke me up late at night with another plate of noodles. He was smiling and said, "siu yeh," midnight snack.

It didn't become a nightly ritual because there were times when Father came straight home from being with George Lee. On other nights, if he felt lucky or needed company, he would stop by a social club, a polite term for gambling den. He would play a few rounds of mahjong, with which he was already familiar from because of playing with Lillian Lee's circle, or fantan, a card game. If he won money, he would celebrate by going to the New Chung King restaurant, which was open late at night, and bring home chow mein, or dried garlic spare ribs or other snack items. Those are the fondest memories I have of Father.

My Grandfather

Father once told me that his father had been a chef on a trans-Pacific steamer but that before that he had worked at a restaurant in the county capital of Sekki; whenever he could, he taught my father how to cook. One day, Grandfather, on one of his many trips across the Pacific, stepped ashore in Hawaii and met a number of the fellow villagers. Apparently the climate in Hawaii was very similar to that in Lung Tow Wan and for the Zhongshan people it was preferable to the village, which was undergoing a famine and raids from neighbouring warlords. Grandfather promised father that on the next trip they would leave the village, board the steamer, and go to Hawaii to make a new home.

Father was excited at the prospect. He had just married and was expecting his first child. They waited anxiously for Grandfather to return home and when he did, he promised to take them with him on the next trip to Hawaii, but that night, Grandfather went to the local teahouse, got into an argument, and was killed. His identity papers were stolen; whoever killed him was desperate to take his place on the trans-Pacific steamer. Father said those were chaotic times in China because of the famine and the constant badgering from warlords and bandits.

It was a crushing blow to Father and his wife. As he told me later, "When I looked out at the river that flowed by my house, there were no fish because the water level was so low. The rice fields next to the house turned dry: there was no water, so there was no crop. We couldn't support ourselves with what we had, and if only your grandfather hadn't met his fate, we'd be in Hawaii now." Father's dream died with his father and he had no choice but go to Gold Mountain to support his family. And that was how he came to Canada.

WORSHIP OF ANCESTORS

Once a year, in early April, the Chinese community takes part in a ceremony called Ching Ming, which literally means "clear and pure brightness." It is also known as All Souls Day, when we go to the cemetery and remember our ancestors. In the early days in the Chinese section of the cemetery, there was a permanent barbecue pit where families cooked a side of pork or chickens to prepare a meal for the departed. Incense sticks and oranges and a dish of the cooked meal were offered to the dead and placed near the headstones. Nowadays the practice is to place flowers and to bow reverently three times before the headstones. The result is that there is a cheerful carpet of flowers in the Chinese section of the cemetery. It's as if an artist had dipped his paint brush into his palette and dotted his canvas with various shades of snowdrops, saffron, and vermillion on an expansive grassy landscape.

After Mother's death, Father started the ritual of worshipping her spirit. On the anniversary of her death, he took Mother's framed photograph from the wall and arranged a temporary altar. On either side of the picture, he burned three incense sticks. In front were three cups of tea. At first I thought they were for the three of us, but instead they were for Heaven, Earth, and Man. After bowing three times and pouring a tiny drop from the cups on the floor, Father took a stack of Chinese funeral money and carefully lit them with a match inside a metal bucket. The money was for Mother to spend in heaven. The rest of our dinner was spent in quiet contemplation.

CHINESE OPERA ON COLUMBIA STREET

Father sometimes took me to the old Chinese Opera House on Columbia, around the corner from Pender Street. It was the only one left after fire destroyed the other opera house on Shanghai Alley. The theatre was small and always crowded. Chinese operas are notoriously long; they last four to six hours. Most of the time when Father and I arrived, we would find his friends and they would chat while the opera carried on. The women brought knitting with them and gossiped amongst themselves. The aisles, well, actually the entire floor, was covered with melon seed or peanut shells. You could hear the cracking of the shells as people walked on them or children ran through them. I used to run up and down the aisles with my friends, ignoring what was happening on stage. Most of the time the music was overwhelming, but we couldn't care less. It was funny when we ran into the lobby and people started to shush us. You would have thought that they would have wanted to be quiet in the auditorium rather than in the lobby.

Tickets purchased at the start of an opera were expensive but became cheaper as the hours went on. One day, Father took my brother Git to the theatre early. After a couple of hours, he took Git's ticket, excused himself, and went out, explaining to the clerk in the box office that he would be back. He went home, told me to put my jacket on, and walked me back to the theatre. He flashed two tickets to the clerk, who waved us in. It was fine as long as he had a ticket for me.

Both my parents had performed in Chinese opera. My brother, Wah, remembered that when he was ten years old he went backstage with Mother at the theatre on Columbia Street. He said it was fascinating to see the actors put on their make-up and costumes. As he watched Mother with her make-up, someone tapped him on the shoulder. He turned to see a monstrous and fierce-looking face and screamed at the top of his lungs. It was the Monkey King with shiny oil make-up on his face. The actor laughed as Mother scolded him and held my trembling brother in her arms.

Jennie said that Mother joined the Chinese opera at the right time. In the days of imperial China, no women had been allowed on stage so men played the roles of women characters. This rule changed with the revolution and from 1912 on, women were allowed on stage. My parents thought it was fun to take advantage of this change. Father volunteered to play the fair maiden while Mother played the ruthless General, a strong male role, which I understand she relished. She wore very large costumes with large pennants sticking out from the back. They represented the number of kingdoms the general had conquered. The more pennants there were, the more powerful the general. Despite these insights into the stories, my only impression of the operas was that they were very loud and difficult to understand. As an adult, I appreciate them more, but you know, it's no fun to see them with clean floors and not being able to run up and down the aisle and chat with friends.

My Brothers

I have one strong memory of my eldest brother, Git, who was sixteen years older than I was. One day, I woke up with a fever and felt awful. I was to attend kindergarten, but with a fever, it was impossible. There was a knock on the door from a classmate with whom I normally walked to school. Git answered the door and I heard him say that I wasn't feeling well and to please tell the teacher. I was grateful and fell back to sleep. Not long afterwards in 1944, Git died of tuberculosis. He was only twenty-two; his ambition had been to become a cook so he had apprenticed for several years and worked up to a short order cook position at a café at English Bay.

When my other brother Wah, who was twelve years older than me, was in high school he took a job working as a grocery clerk in New Westminster. Father scoffed at the idea and tried to convince him to work closer to home but Wah insisted. It was a weekend job, just perfect for a high school student. On Friday after school, he would take the interurban tram, stay overnight at the store, and work Saturday and Sunday from eight in the morning until midnight for a dollar a day. His boss was a kindly Chinese man and knew my father. A year later when he attended university, Wah worked at another grocery store but closer to home. It was on Hastings and Abbott, across from Woodward's department store. A Chinese girl who attended the same Chinese language school, and eventually the same university, also worked along side with him.

Father told me later in life that he didn't want Wah to go to war in 1944. Wah was eighteen and the Canadian government was conscripting young men from the Chinese community, but 1944 was also when our eldest brother, Git, died of tuberculosis. Pop was heartbroken; it only seemed like yesterday when he had attended my mother's funeral. He didn't want to risk losing his next oldest son, so he encouraged Wah to attend university in the hope of keeping him out of the military.

At the University of British Columbia (UBC), Wah won many scholarships. Father was very proud and often, he reported the news to the Chinese newspapers and clipped out the articles that were written about Wah. Father was even prouder when Wah worked for UNICEF at the New York headquarters for two years and became a career man assigned to posts in Pakistan, Thailand, the Philippines, and India. Also during his time at UBC, Wah became president of the Chinese Varsity Club and told me that one day, he went through the membership list and decided to date all the girls in alphabetical order. Wah was always a neat dresser, a trait picked up from Father. On a date, he wore a clean shirt and tie, a suit, and if the weather was cold, a camelhair overcoat. He always ironed his shirts and folded them like Father did for the

Father with brothers Wah and Git

Brother Wah in VJ Day (Victory over Japan Day) parade holding the Russian flag

Brother Wah and Vivian meeting the President of the Philippines, Ferdinand Marcos, at an official function

shirts he made. After receiving his Master's degree in the United States, Wah eventually married Vivian, also a Master's graduate from the United States. You know funnily enough, Vivian not only was the Chinese girl with whom Wah attended Chinese language school, university, and worked with at the grocery store, she was also the last name on his list.

THE FIRST CHINESE DISK JOCKEY

After kindergarten, my sister Jennie encouraged me to attend Sunday school, which led to me to join the Cubs at the old YWCA, then a storefront near Gore Avenue. Jennie attended the Y, too, as a member of the Moongate Players, an amateur theatre group. She was also active in a teen group called Teen Town sponsored by the *Vancouver Sun*.

I have to credit Jennie for introducing me to the library across the street because without her help, I wouldn't have been interested in literature. The first book she wanted me to read was about *King Arthur and the Round Table*. The next book was *The Wooden Horse*, a story about prisoners of war in World War Two escaping from a German camp, much like *The Great Escape*. A librarian recommended that book to me, and it initiated my love of reading.

At school, Jennie met a girl with buckteeth who was anxious to get into show business, thanks to her mother, Bunny. Mimi was vivacious and talented. She started her singing career in a vaudeville show at a theatre on Hastings near Main. It was called the Stage, and Mimi in years to come partnered with an America nightclub performer named Phil Ford. They became a comedy team with the name of Mimi Hines and Phil Ford. When Mimi replaced Barbra Streisand on Broadway in the musical "Funny Girl," she invited Jennie to be her guest in New York City.

One day Jennie entered a contest as part of a fundraising effort to build a new YWCA building in downtown Vancouver. Imagine her surprise when she won. The prize was a six-month stint as a disk jockey with a program on the radio. She was on the air Saturday afternoons broadcasting a half-hour program from CKMO. She played music and, best of all, interviewed the celebrities who came to Vancouver and entertained at various nightclubs. She was the first Chinese disk jockey in Vancouver. Later, she ran a make-up business in Edmonton and became a minor celebrity herself.

WHEN MY SISTER WAS DISOWNED AND OWNED AGAIN

It was not long after Wah left home for Seattle that Jennie also left. She didn't finish her year at King George High School even though she was active with the Chinese YWCA and Teen Town. Like Wah, she had had enough of Chinatown. She was caught between being a good Chinese girl in Chinatown and being a young woman who wanted to explore the world outside China-town. So one day she made up her mind and left.

She went to Atikokan, Ontario, and settled there, working as a sales clerk. On her frequent trips to the butcher shop, she met a friendly butcher who she charmed. She wrote letters to me and assured me not to worry about her. One day, she announced she was getting married to the butcher, whose name was Garry Diment. When I passed on this information to Father, he hit the roof and immediately disowned Jennie. He was furious. I guess it wouldn't have been so bad if she had married a Chinese, but a lo fan, a Caucasian! He ranted on and on, swearing to his friends that she was no longer his daughter. No one, but no one, in his family had ever married a non-Chinese. He was hurt, of course, and confused. How could a daughter do such a thing? Hadn't he provided her with a roof over her head? Clothing? Food? He really didn't understand. He had had enough problems trying to keep in touch with First Wife and his son in revolutionary China and was just barely recovering from the death of his second wife and second son.

Eventually my sister returned home and introduced her hus-band. Father, still smarting from a marriage he did not approve of,

Portrait of Jennie in 1960

put on a brave face and set his differences aside. That afternoon, they were to arrive, he prepared a special meal. It was not a sweet and sour or a chop suey dinner that most lo fan would expect in restaurants in the 1950s. Nor was it Chinese banquet style. Instead, he cooked what he did best. There were steamed salted fish, sautéed Chinese pickled greens with beef, steamed minced pork pie with duck yolk, and slivers of preserved turnips, roasted chicken with garlic, and steamed rice. In short, he prepared old-fashioned village or peasant type dishes.

Father greeted his new son-in-law with a smile though the questions must have been racing through his mind: Is he really good enough for my daughter? Can he hold a job? Will he treat my daughter respectfully?

"What do you do?" asked my father.

"I work as a butcher," said Garry.

Ah, thought my father. *A butcher. There'll always be a need for butchers. He'll never be out of a job. Good.*

He poured Garry a glass of Johnny Walker's Red Label. They clinked glasses and toasted a good marriage. I looked at my father and was surprised to see how pleasant he was. What a difference from when he had first heard the news of the marriage.

As we sat at the dinner table, both father and Jennie helped Garry from the serving dishes. He ate everything with gusto. I'm sure Father arched one eyebrow. Years later, when I asked Jennie about the dinner, she laughed at the memory of it and reminded me of the "care" packages that I sent her. When Garry was court-ing her, she tried cooking from her memories of watching Father cook, but she didn't have the proper food like preserved turnips, ginger roots and five spice powder. Some ingredients she pur-chased in Atikokan weren't the same as in Vancouver, so she sent a shopping list to me. I gladly bought and mailed the items she requested. Garry was game and enjoyed her cooking; it was dif-ferent from his usual fare and more important, it was tasty. By the time he met Father, he was familiar with Chinese food, so it was no surprise to Jennie that he ate every morsel at dinner.

In more than one way, my sister was a pioneer. When I think about it now, it's remarkable that Jennie could marry a non-Chinese person in the late 1940s when it wasn't acceptable, let alone common. She is one of those women who can count a number of firsts in her life.

LIVING IN THE BACK OF A STORE

Father and I slept in a loft above his working space at the back of the store. He had enough room for a brass bed, while I had to contend with a mattress on the floor. There was a ladder to the loft, and in time, because he was getting old, my father slept on top of his worktable downstairs. I didn't get to sleep in the brass bed, but I was used to the mattress. Before that I had slept in an old metal baby crib with high sides.

Father had a canary in a cage on a stand. Once a day he fed the bird and was rewarded with cheerful singing. He was careful that the canary had enough seeds, water, and a piece of white chalk. Once a week or more, he would clean the bottom of the cage by taking away the old newspaper and replacing it with a new one. The canary was soothing for the store. Against the sound from Father's sewing machine and his buttonhole machine going all day long, the tweeting of the canary was a relief.

Then there was my brother, who took violin lessons when he was attending Grandview Commerce School. He wanted to play in the school orchestra. At that time the Louie family lived in an apartment above us. Their children were the same age as Wah and Jennie. Wah took his lessons at his teacher's house and practised every evening at home. He eventually made it as a violin player in the school orchestra so he practised even more, particularly a very difficult passage which he had to repeat over and over. I can picture the Louie family with their hands to their ears running and screaming into the night to get away from my brother's screeching violin. By coincidence, the Louie family moved out of the apartment shortly after.

AFFINITY WITH GLASS

When I was a child, glass seemed to have an inexplicable attraction to me. I was five years old when a strange incident took place at home. In my home, the living quarters were partitioned from the business side by a curtain. Father's workbench was in the living quarters right against the partition where there was an opening for him to look out when he was behind his Singer sewing machine.

One side of the store had two large wall display cases, and I was short enough that my head could rest on the ledge that separated the display above from the covered storage space below. Each cabinet was wooden and was painted a chocolate brown and each had two sliding glass doors that ran on tracks on the top and bottom ledges. Behind the glass, on glass shelves were bolts of cloth, and tailored shirts in their opened boxes.

Occasionally Father would push the doors in such a way that they slammed against the frame, rattled loudly, and quivered in their tracks. I loved the noise so I played with the doors by sliding them back and forth on their tracks, much to Father's annoyance. Across from the wall cabinets were two floor display cases that also served as counters. Inside them were two glass shelves holding more shirts and other men's wear such as ties, handkerchiefs, and socks. The display cases reminded me of the ones in the museum. If I stood on my toes and stretched my arms up, I could just barely reach the top of the counter with my fingers. Between the wall and the floor displays, I had enough room to play cowboys and Indians by running around in circles. The red concrete floor was hard on my feet but if it were rainy outside, I didn't mind.

On the occasion I'm recalling, my whooping and yelling must have irritated my sister, who was busy reading a comic book as she sat comfortably on the living room sofa. She called me from behind the curtained entrance but I ignored her. She called a second and a third time, the last time with a hard edge to her voice. I looked up and could see my Father's head bent over the sewing machine. Reluctantly, I stopped playing and sauntered over to my sister. I was just stepping into the curtained entrance when I heard a sharp crack behind my back, followed by a crashing sound of wood and glass. The shattering noise held my feet to the floor, and as the clinking faded, I turned around to see what had happened.

One large glass sliding door had come off the top track and toppled over the floor display case. Jagged pieces of glass from the remains of the counter stood on the fallen door, which was mutilated by glass and wood splinters. The bottom frame of the door was broken at the foot of the wall display case, leaving a fractured ledge with raw wood. Glass fragments were strewn over the shirts and the floor.

Father stopped his Singer and rushed out to me. His hands reached my shoulders and turned me to face him as he knelt. The curtain of the entranceway fluttered from his rush and I could see Jennie sitting wordlessly on the sofa. "Are you all right?" he said. I was trembling but I managed a nod. In a rare display of affection, he hugged me and I felt him turn his head to ask my sister, "What made you call out to him?"

"I don't know," she said. "I don't know. Something made me do it. I don't know why. I just called out." Father held me away with outstretched arms, and looked at me for a long time. Finally he said, "Your mother's spirit is looking after you." Later there were similar incidents in which I escaped from harm, and though I can't explain it, I think Father was right.

My second story is about something that happened when I was fourteen. I was on my way to visit Wesley, who lived with his parents on the top floor of a three-storey walk-up apartment. The building was long and narrow from the alley to the street. The entrance was on the east side. A sidewalk with a wooden railing marked the boundary of the property. You could enter the building from either the alley way or the street.

I came from the alley and walked under an overhang where part of the building jutted over the sidewalk. I passed a large window and three storeys above was my friend's living room window. Then I pushed the front entrance door and walked up three flights of stairs. As I reached the landing and started to knock there was a crash and tinkling of glass. At that same moment, Mrs. Woo, Wesley's mother, opened the door and said, "What the heck?"

I entered the apartment and shook my head. Wesley came out of his room to greet me and noticed the fluttering of the curtains by the window.

"Jeez, Ma," he said. "The window's gone."

The three of us peered through the open space where the window had once been. On the ground, against the railing and covered with broken glass and shards, was the smashed wooden frame. Somehow the sash had come loose, and the window tumbled down to the spot where I had been only a few seconds earlier.

SONNY

Sometimes I'd invite my friend Sonny to the store. He's now known as Wayson Choy. We spent quite a bit of time after school at his house, as well as at the library across the street from my father's store and, of course, went to the movies together. One day his mother dropped in and introduced herself to Father. She knew me, of course. They chatted for a long time and when it was time for her to leave, she turned around and said to Father, "What a good boy."

My father smiled. "She decided to come and find out what kind of parent I am because she knows what kind of a son you are." I guess it was typical of families in Chinatown to know who everyone was and to whom the children belonged. Mrs. Choy knew practically everyone in Chinatown. She worked at a Chinese sausage factory during the day and played in a mahjong circle with the ladies at night.

One day, after Sonny and I had played with my movie projector and he had left for home, Father, who was at the sewing machine, turned to me and said, "You know, he's an adopted boy, but don't tell him that." Many years later, at the age of fifty-five, Wayson did find out that he was adopted, and asked me if I knew anything about it. I told him no. I felt obliged to keep my word to Father, I suppose you could say out of filial piety, but many years later, I eventually told Wayson about my promise to Father, that yes, I knew he was adopted. In his memoir, *Paper Shadows*, Wayson mentions this incident. I believe Father would have forgiven me for breaking my promise.

FATHER'S FRIENDS AND VISITORS

Father had a number of friends. I remember there were two old gentlemen, short and almost bald with wrinkles and sunken cheeks. Their eyes crinkled when they laughed as they tapped their feet at Father's funny stories. During the winter, they rarely visited the store together. It didn't occur to me that they must

Portrait of Wayson, mid 1950s

have had only one heavy woollen jacket between the two of them until Jennie pointed it out. I think she was right. They lived in New Westminster, some twelve miles away by the interurban train. The Chinese referred to New Westminster as Yee Foal or Second City. The interurban used trains powered by electricity from an overhead wire. As in Vancouver, it was a short walk from Chinatown in New Westminster to the interurban station. The sawmills and canneries attracted the Chinese to New Westminster and, for a short while, the Chinatown there was larger than the one in Vancouver. The two old men who visited Father worked as labourers, and on their days off travelled to Chinatown in Vancouver to visit friends and relatives, and to shop for food. Like most Chinese, they had no telephone, and travel by tram was the only way to keep in touch. I always called them Gung Gung which meant "Grandfather," but whether they really were or not, I don't know. It was the practice in Chinatown to foster family titles for close friends.

Sometimes, titles can be confusing. There was another visitor, tall and thin with sunken cheeks who always wore a heavy dark woollen checked jacket and a porkpie hat. I called him Cow Fool, Chinese for "Maternal Uncle," and for a very long time, I really thought he was Mother's brother. However, he was really the brother of Father's First Wife. All children borne by second and successive wives are considered to belong to the First Wife. Cow Fool had a very distinctive bearing. He stood ramrod straight and sat up straight in his chair. He gave me treats such as small packets of red ginger, preserved plums, or beef jerky. I learned that he drank a glass of whisky each day. He claimed it warded off colds and germs and kept his heart and lungs alert and live.

We called him Cow Fool or maternal uncle

"Doctor" was the name of another visitor. I don't think he was a real doctor but that was what he called. He was a tall man, thin with very dark hair, his face usually unshaven. He always wore a fedora and a light-coloured suit with a tie. In the winter, he wore a beautiful camel hair overcoat. He and Father discussed politics, particularly General Chiang Kai-shek who had retreated to the island of Formosa and was waiting to take back mainland China from the Communists. Like most residents of Chinatown, they were keen to have the Kuomintang Party return to their homeland. This was especially true in the early fifties when the Communists seized letters from overseas Chinese for the addresses. They knew Father's generation sent money on a monthly basis to the home village and now they wrote back threatening letters demanding more money. The blackmail angered many in the Chinese community but there was no choice if they wanted to keep their relatives in China alive.

F.P.

Of all of Father's friends, F.P. was my favourite. F.P.'s real name was Gum Sing: we addressed him in Chinese as Gum Sing Baak, "Baak" being a Chinese term for a man over sixty years of age. For a long time, I accepted the name F.P. but one day I asked my brother, "What the heck does F.P. stand for?"

"Easy," said Wah. "Friend of Pop's."

F.P. lived in the Li Kiu Hotel on Pender Street, the same hotel where my parents had lived when my eldest brother, Git, was born. He was a very close friend of the family and, in many ways, a babysitter and a second father, even though he was not from the same village. F.P. came from a village further south and east from an area called Toishan, and had worked as a houseboy and had other various jobs in mills until he was unable to continue. He had thinning hair and fair skin, and his shaven face was always scrubbed clean. His clothes were also clean if not new, usually a suit with a shirt and tie. He was particular about cleanliness and often criticized Father for not being a good housekeeper. Father, in the course of making a shirt, cut cloth materials and often bits and pieces fell to the floor and would lie there until the end of the day when he would sweep them up. Sometimes however, he was in a hurry or too busy and left the floor until the next day.

Father almost always prepared dinner for us, and we would eat and clean up before F.P. came into the store. Father trusted him with a key to it. They would greet and chat with each other and finally Father would leave us to help his friend, George Lee, at his confectionery store on Hastings Street. F.P. as a babysitter took me out for walks. On our walks, F.P. told me stories about the early Chinese labourers who had worked on the railway. He had met some of them in Chinatown when he first came to Vancouver in the 1900s. They had come from the same Toishan district as he had.

While listening to his stories, we would walk north on Main Street to the Canadian National Steamship quay. We would cross Hastings Street, go past the Star Theatre, a movie house that showed old movies, walk by the police station, pass Cordova Street where a large concrete building housed the International Seafarers Union, and then stroll past a string of small stores that stretched to Powell Street, where on the corner was Chut Goo, a woman who ran a barber shop.

Father always took me to a lady barber on Powell Street. Mrs. Fung ran a shop that had two barber chairs and half a dozen regular chairs. She was a nice woman and Father enjoyed talking to her while she cut my hair. There was also another lady barber, Mrs. Anna Leong, who was a close friend of Mother's. Mrs. Leong and my mother had attended the Moler School of Hairdressing on West Hastings Street near the cenotaph at Victory Square. Mrs. Leong went on to apprentice with a shop in Chinatown while Mother used what she learned by helping with the hair and wig make-up for Chinese operas. Since they both came from the same village or district as Father, they spoke the same dialect. Also, as Mrs. Fung and Mrs. Leong were nearby so I ended up going from one to the other for my haircuts, and they didn't seem to mind. I think they were among the first women barbers.

Larry with F.P.

The next street over was Alexander, where F.P. and I climbed the steep pedestrian ramp above the Canadian Pacific Railway tracks. If we were on time, we gazed towards the west where a puff of white smoke signalled that the eastbound train was ready to pull out of the station from the foot of Granville Street. We once watched the train from overhead, but the fumes from the steam engine were stingingly hot and smelly. It was better to stand on the street level to watch the passing train.

Minutes later, the railway crossing signals flashed red and bells clanged while the barriers swung down on the side streets and there was a series of whistles from the train as the giant steam locomotive roared into sight and chugged past, the engineer waving from his cab window. I waved back, filled with envy and thrilled that he was going across the country. The ground was still shaking while the passenger cars click-clacked away.

Sometimes, we went to the nearby North Vancouver dock to watch the hustle of the ferry unloading and loading passengers and cars. We admired the *S.S. Prince George* that was tied up at the pier waiting for the next sailing up the BC coast. Across the way was a fish cannery and occasionally we saw workers taking coffee breaks. Other times we watched seiners unload their catch while overhead the seagulls wheeled and screamed their delight.

We also often walked to Chinatown to visit F.P.'s cousin, the butcher. I remember the smell of sawdust on the floor and the chill that came from the cooler room. Mr. Sing always had a kind word for me, and was generous in slicing a piece of pork or beef, wrapping it up in Kraft paper, and saying, "Here, give this to your father and say hello for me."

At home, because we had no hot running water, every Sunday F.P. would fetch me at the store and take me up the street to his hotel. Going through the outer swinging doors, we climbed the steps from the sidewalk to the first floor, past the front desk and up another two flights of stairs around a square light well and halfway down the hallway was his room. It had a wash basin, a single bed, a set of drawers, a closet, and a couple of wooden tables covered with paper bags, both small and large shopping bags that were full. One of the bags leaned against a can of tobacco. I peeped in and saw pieces of cloth material from Father's. For some reason, F.P. was collecting them. He would fetch a couple of towels and take me down to the end of the hallway where there was a bathtub. It was iron, deep, and stood on four legs that looked like claws. F.P. would draw the bath while I undressed. The bath was always hot and F.P. helped scrub me clean until I was able to do it by myself.

F.P. was a smoker who rolled his own cigarettes from a tin of tobacco and a packet of cigarette paper. He was skilled in rolling with two hands; the tobacco held firm in the hand rolled tube. Then he'd light up with a wooden match and I never failed to inhale the pungent odour of sulphur as it flared up after the strike against the sandpaper strip on the match box. It always amused me when he blew smoke rings much to his delight.

One sad day half way through my high school years, I noticed a subtle change over him. Father was a barometer for F.P., and soon he began to gently shoo F.P. away.

"Why did you do that for?" I asked.

"Son," he said. "He's very ill. Don't go near him anymore."

"But why Father, why?"

"Never you mind," he said. "Do as I say. Don't go near him." The next night, F.P. opened the door, but just as quickly, father took him outside. The third night, my father, to my surprise, snatched the key from F.P.

"Don't let him in," he said, "if he comes again."

I nodded. Father always knew what he was doing.

Something in F.P.'s mind snapped. For a month he came to the door to the usual time of the evening and knocked when he found he had no key. I sat alone in the house, mute to the fading knocks, terrified at some great fear. Each night I peered out the window. I saw that F.P. was increasingly slovenly in appearance, and his back bent more forward until it was almost parallel to the ground. When I had enough courage, I followed him, and to my surprise, he started to rummage through the garbage cans in the alleyway. From the cans he took pieces of newspapers, then folded and carried them under his arms. I followed him back to his hotel and watched the bent old man climbing the stairs that I once knew so well, back to his room.

One day, a friend came to the house and said that the police had found F.P. in a box car out in the freight yards. Father rushed to the police station but all he received from the old man was meaningless babble. F.P. must have wandered in the streets, and finding himself lost, took refuge in a box car in the nearby rail freight yard, content to spend the night there. F.P. did not recognize Father but he instantly thanked him.

One evening when I was just about ready to go out on a date, he knocked on the door. He greeted me, saying how much I have grown. Somehow I thought he was all right again and to make him feel welcome, I asked him how my dress pants looked. He looked at me and said, "You look fine but ah, I see, your cuffs." He bent down and rolled my pant legs halfway up my knees. "There, that's better," he said. We stood silently for a moment, awkwardly, well, at least I felt awkward. I wished silently that someone, anyone, would come in. I closed my eyes: perhaps he would vanish, disappear. Childish magic. His hand touched me. I thanked him and led him back into the streets and closed the door behind him, aware he would never be the old F.P. I told my father about the incident and he said, "Well, my son, I'm afraid he has gone mad. He has the mind of a simple idiot. No, I don't know why."

In the hot month of August, F.P. died sitting on the curb outside the hotel. At this news, father spat on the floor. "The crazy fool," he said. "The crazy fool. Didn't I tell you, son, he's gone mad." Then he laughed, and I became disgusted with him. How could my father laugh at the death of his best friend?

There were only five of us at the funeral. I remember Father standing by the open coffin and smiling. At the cemetery we stood in the hot sun while the minister droned on. When he finished, we each took a handful of dirt and sprinkled F.P.'s coffin.
I looked up. Father's face was etched with wrinkles I never saw before. I did not cry until late at night when I was alone.

After the funeral, Father and I had to go to his hotel room to collect F.P.'s possessions. The room was crowded with boxes of papers and bottles. His desk was littered with tiny Chinese medicine bottles and his bed worn with a sag in the middle outlining his figure. While we were cleaning the room, we heard knocking outside in the hallway. Thinking it was F.P.'s door, I opened it, only to see a heavily made up woman across the hallway being admitted by a boarder. I suddenly saw F.P., surrounded by loneliness, with no one to visit or a place to call home, or worse, someone to love. Suddenly I felt small. My father saw my face; he put his arms around me and we walked out of the room without a word.

OUR NEIGHBOURS

Our store was the middle one of three. On our right was a secondhand furniture store run by a Jewish family. They had two daughters, one about the same age as Jennie; the other was a year younger than I was. The little girl often came over to visit us.

Jennie tells a story about the little girl returning to her family who asked, "Did you have anything to eat next door?" and she replied, "Yes."

"What, dear?"

"Pork!!" came the answer. We can just imagine the look of horror on their faces.

Another time, she came to visit and being very curious about sex and life in general, I took her to our bathroom, which was literally a water closet. It was a small room with only a toilet. Behind closed doors, we took off our clothes and looked at each other. "What's that?" she asked, pointing to my weenie. I told her. "When do I get it?" she asked. Not knowing a single thing about sex and thinking that she would grow one as she got older, I said, "Oh, when you get older." I smirk to myself every time I think about that experience. My naïve answer gave way to a far different meaning later in adult life.

On the other side of us was Granny's Market, a store run by a stout white-haired woman who always wore a blue smock and was called Granny. She really did look like a granny, and spoke with a slight French accent. She told me she had come from Madagascar a long time ago. Her store was part chocolate shop, part ice cream shop, and part novelty shop. She used to get cartons of chocolate, all in paper wrappers. She would sort the chocolates in small boxes for sale. For the fancy ones, she tied a nice red ribbon. They were mostly the creamy type of chocolate, which I didn't really care for, but her ice cream was really nice. It came from Hazelwood Creamery on Keefer Street, the same place where we used to get our block of ice for the ice box. Granny also sold musical boxes, kewpie dolls, knick knacks, cigarettes and newspapers. Jennie was given several kewpie dolls but they all had blond hair and blue eyes, and she wished there were dolls for Chinese girls.

Granny had a helper named Nelson. He was a middle-aged man who spoke with a Scottish accent, and wore a clean shirt and pants every day. I think he did the paperwork and legwork for Granny. He was always running errands and I suppose he did some deliveries too. In the fall, he would be in the backyard chopping firewood. Like us, Granny and Nelson had a woodburning stove and kept their firewood in a shed.

The walls between the stores were thin. I remember lying on my mattress in the loft at night and hearing Granny's radio. There was a reason why she had the radio on at eleven at night. It was for a radio program called "Roy Ward Dickson Doghouse," which started each night with a person whistling followed by a dog barking. There was loud music and, in between, the reason why Granny was listening: she was one of the sponsors and advertised her shop on the show.

One summer evening, I was arguing with Father, who continued to shout at me in an increasingly loud voice. That shut me up, but nevertheless I had continued sulking by the time Granny appeared at the door. By then, Father sat in his chair, his back to me.

"I can hear you arguing from next door," she said.

Father grunted and avoided looking at her.

"Listen," she said to me. "You should listen to your father."

I could see the back of Father's head raised ever so slightly and nodded.

"You go and put your arms around your father and let him know you appreciate him."

I didn't move.

"Go on," she urged.

It was my turn to grunt.

"Go on," she continued.

I placed my arms around Father. He was motionless in his chair. "Now hug him."

What Granny didn't realize was that as in most Asian families, particularly in my case, Father did not show affection openly. To touch was out of the question, but hug him, well, I did, for the first time. I think at that time, if Father had enough English vocabulary, he would have said, "Lady, for God's sake, back off."

"There, you see," said Granny. "That wasn't hard."

I managed to smile at Granny, who left just as quickly as she appeared in our store.

Steamed Buns
chicken, barbeque, pork

SCHOOL DAYS

At first, my eldest brother Git escorted me to school, and when he was confident I could walk the three-block distance I would go alone at eight-thirty in the morning. In the spring, the sun would be up and shopkeepers would be opening their shutters, cranking down their canvas awnings, and hosing their sidewalks, getting ready for the day. Huge trucks parked on the street as swampers unloaded the crates to waiting workers at the produce stores who opened the contents of farm-fresh vegetables and fruits. Poultry clerks wheeled stacks of coops filled with squawking white and brown chickens out onto the sidewalk. The chickens took much of the sidewalk space in front of the poultry shop so I either had to walk around them or onto the pavement to avoid the stench and feathers that drifted in the air.

I attended the Chinese United Church kindergarten on Dunlevy Street, a two-block walk from Main Street. Looking at my graduation picture of 1945, I recognise the teachers, Lily McCargar, Isabel Montgomery, and Marion Mah, who now are all gone. Of the fifteen students, I have kept in touch intermittently over the last fifty-four years with Sonny, Raymond, Ken, and Nancy. Of the group, Sonny, or Wayson Choy the novelist, is the most well known. Others, such as Phyllis, Donna, and Lucie are still in Vancouver.

Pender Street didn't change much when I attended grade school. My first teacher was Miss Barbara. She was a good and kind lady who looked after us well in Grade 1. Miss Laverock was another teacher. It was routine to arrive at the homeroom and wait with the class for our teacher. As soon as she arrived and said, "Good morning, class," we quickly got up and stood by our desks and responded in unison, "Good morning, Miss Laverock," then recited the Lord's Prayer before sitting down. Miss Laverock was a Scottish lady who always wore her hair in a bun and dressed immaculately in a tan-coloured suit. She spoke with a slight Scottish accent and I never actually heard her speak in anger. My favourite teacher in my eight years at elementary school was Eileen Farrington. She was a tall woman with honey-coloured hair done

Chinese United Church Kindergarten in 1945. Larry at second from left in the back row. Wayson at second from the right in the back row

up in a French roll. She wore glasses, but what was outstanding was her clothing. She always wore a white blouse with a red vest and a long black skirt. As a teacher she was the embodiment of goodness and grace. She was also generous in opening her house for one-day visits in the summer. Unfortunately, I felt ashamed of living in Chinatown and was shy about going to a better part of the city.

In Grade 3, I got into a fistfight with a young Quebecois named Raymond. One of us was in the wrong seat and refused to yield. Raymond was a tough kid and spoke tough, too, and I guess I didn't like his manners. We threw punches at each other and grappled on the floor. Eventually our classmates separated us just as our teacher was coming down the hallway. Looking back on the incident now, I can see that he must have really felt like a stranger in our English speaking class and had done what he could to protect himself.

My Strathcona neighbourhood was a mixture of Jewish, Russian, Ukrainian, Black, Italian, Japanese, and Chinese. Billy, John, and Gino were Italian, David was Japanese, John was Russian, Reggie was Black, Jim was Ukrainian, Larry was Irish, Morris was Jewish, and I, Chinese. There were also Milton and Wesley, both Chinese as well. Also, there was "Farmer," a nickname we had for a blond sturdy Russian boy. I'm not sure why we called him Farmer but he didn't seem to mind. Another was a dark-haired Italian we called "Minnow" because his last name was Minichiello. There were the Nishi boys, David and Gordy. And there was my good friend Wes Woo. Once there was a classmate named Larry Kelly, who had red hair and freckles. We got along famously and visited each other's homes. Larry was surprised I lived in the back of a store. Later, I found out that his mother had moved to a houseboat under the Burrard Bridge, and that was the last I saw of Larry.

We were all children of immigrants, and we all respected each other's differences and got along: we couldn't care less what background we came from. By visiting each other, we got a sense of different cultures and languages, but these things were not important then. Friendship was what mattered. Sometimes there were fights but nothing serious. One joy of such a mixed group was being invited to each other's house or, better yet, to dinner. John Minichiello lived across the street from the school. His house was huge and one day his mother invited me for dinner. I don't remember what was on the table except that his father offered me a glass of his homemade red wine. That was my introduction to wine and I must have enjoyed it as I still remember the occasion.

A number of Chinese students became prominent as adults and my contemporaries were no exception. I remember when Milton Wong was first elected class president at Strathcona School and awarded the Citizenship Award at the end of Grade 8. This revealed his potential as demonstrated when he was Chancellor of Simon Fraser University, and won other honours.

PLAYING HOOKY

School became routine and I didn't really care for it. There were days when the weather was so warm and the sky so blue, it took a real effort to go to school, so one time, I thought to myself, I'll skip school today. I took a long way through several blocks to avoid being seen by any friends of Father's until I reached the foot of Columbia Street, where the North Vancouver ferry was docked. The ferry carried cars and passengers back and forth across Burrard Inlet.

I joined the line-up of adults, and being so small, ducked under the gaze of the lady in the ticket booth and walked up the ramp and scampered up the stairs to the passenger lounge where there were benches and a coffee bar. Some of the crew looked at me but I looked the other way and they left me alone.

On the crossing of Burrard Inlet, I imagined myself sailing off to some far-off exotic world, to places where palm trees swayed in the breeze or to the shores of some mysterious island. What I actually saw were large freighters waiting in the harbour, tugboats pulling barges, and coastal steamships on their way to isolated villages up the coast. Yet it was a thrill to ride the ferry away from the city and watch the receding skyline. I recognized the Sun tower, which resembled an Orange Crush bottle, and the large W on top of the Woodward's building, and further to the west the white and tan Marine Building. There was the Hotel Vancouver with its green, copper-clad roof and by the waterfront the red and white of the CPR station. By the end of the day, I must have gone back and forth at least a dozen times. It was a pleasant way to spend the day and, admittedly, an escape I needed. But school was actually a lot of fun. I had lots of good friends. Some have remained in contact to the present.

MY BIG STAY AT THE HOSPITAL

I contacted tuberculosis at the age of ten. For a respiratory disease, I had it in the strangest place. A lump appeared on the left side of my neck; obviously it was a boil, or so the herbalist told Father. I had to wear a Chinese equivalent of a shinplaster, which looked and felt like dried mud mixed with polyfill. The lump refused to go away and as a last resort, Father took me to see a lo fan doctor who when he found out that Mother had died of a combination of TB and asthma, and Git from TB, immediately sent me to St. Paul's hospital for thirty days.

During my hospital stay, Jennie, who knew I was a big cowboy movie fan, encouraged me to write to my favourite cowboy stars in Hollywood for their photographs. I certainly had time to write letters and after the first couple of letters, I was thrilled to receive autographed pictures in return. To this day, I have kept my album of Roy Rogers, Gene Autry, and all the rest of them from the fifties.

My hospital stay coincided with the beginning of a school year, so for the first few weeks I was confined to my bed until I was wheeled into the operating room. It was a frightening experience and I vividly remember the surgeon asking me to take a deep breath as he placed a mask over my face. The sweet smell of the ether soon knocked me out and I felt myself falling into complete darkness. Suddenly a street lamp lit up and a shadowy figure kept asking, "Who's Larry Wong? Who's Larry Wong?" It was the strangest dream I had ever had. When I woke up, I felt a need for nice cold ice cream, which the nurse happily gave me. And I felt something strange on the left side of my neck. It was a dressing held by bandages. The nurse told me not to loosen it and to expect an occasional itchy sensation. I was released in October but had to stay home to recuperate until Christmas, which was just as well. The huge dressing made me very self-conscious.

During this time, my classmates brought me homework to do and helped a lot to keep me up with my schoolwork. My friend George Leung explained my absence to my teacher and so was assigned to bring me homework at the hospital. I found out that TB was common in Chinatown. My doctor told me that the Chinese were susceptible to the disease. One man I knew spent time in a sanatorium near Kamloops. My sister later also contracted the disease, but like me, in a non-respiratory area. I have no doubt we were medical oddities. The miracle drug at that time was an organic compound containing sulphur called sulphanilamide. When I was sent home to recuperate, I was given the new sulpha drugs in the form of 25 brown pills I had to swallow daily.

I returned to school in the New Year and really regretted it. The dressing on my neck drew a lot of stares from classmates. In time, it came off and revealed what I feared most; an ugly scar on my neck that I still have. I was so self-conscious that for the rest of my life I became shy and at times, withdrawn. Much later, I met two European women who, after a glance of my neck, turned and lifted their hair to show similar scars on their necks.

MY EARLY COACH

When I returned to school, the doctor at the hospital who had treated me said I was to avoid physical exertion and should perhaps take up golf in my early twenties. In my junior years at elementary school and in high school, I was excused from gym class and spent time at the library. I had a reputation for being studious in Grade 7 and Grade 8, and ended up with the nickname of "Professor." Of course, by then I was wearing dark frame glasses with thick lenses that contributed to that image.

One day I met Wes Woo. He had just arrived from China, but had been born in Vancouver. His father, a staunch Nationalist, sent him to China right after the war for a classic Chinese education. Wes hated the school, the teachers and the war-torn environment around him. Besides, the school wasn't really ready for students so soon after the war, and so for Wes school was a total waste of time.

As for me, I had to sit out gym class. According to my doctor, I should avoid any physical exertion until I turned 21. By then I could take up golf. My exemption from gym meant I sat on the bench while my classmates played all kinds of sports. Not long after, I was joined by John Minichiello. He suffered from multiple sclerosis, so he, too, had to sit out.

We were in the same class in high school and by then, spent our gym time in the library. Meanwhile, Wes became interested in weight lifting. He bought a set of dumbbells and other equipment so he could train in his bedroom. Eventually he ran out of room because he kept adding to his collection. Not far from where he lived was the Gibbs Boys Club at the Schara Tzedeck synagogue, the first permanent one in Vancouver. The congregation moved away in 1948 and Rufus Gibbs bought the building. He turned it into a gymnasium and and later donated it to the Vancouver Boys' Club Association.

Wes successfully convinced management to allow him to use the basement, which was the beginning of his gym. He believed weight-training was a good way to keep in shape as well as to build strength. He considered it a supplement to major sports, and hated to see me sitting around doing nothing, so he took my under his wings, so to speak, and patiently trained me. He taught me the importance of breathing while exercising as well as the proper movements in weight-lifting. I kept wondering, however, whether my doctor would think I was exerting myself too much!

Wes was as innovative as he was persuasive. When we were in grade school, he had been interested in flying model airplanes. I used to go to the Jong Wah drugstore at the corner of Pender and Gore to buy five-cent airplane model kits. A kit consisted of a thin balsa sheet with wings and rudder stamped on heavy ink for easy attachment to a fuselage. The fuselage was a balsa stick that had to be carved in accordance with instructions and the template in the kit. I never did carve the fuselage the right way and found the whole experience frustrating.

Wes, on the other hand, built a complete fuselage with ribs, wings, moving flaps, a set of wheels, all covered with tissues hiding the intricacy of pulleys and wires. A small .049 cubic inch gasoline engine powered the plane. He flew it on the Strathcona School grounds. The motor was noisy but he could control the plane from take-off to circling around him. One time, he designed an airplane with a pusher propeller that I thought ingenious. He hand carved the propeller with a reverse pitch at the right angle to power his new airplane. Ingenious!

As my coach, Wes entered me in a weightlifting meet when he was confident I had mastered the three Olympic lifts. My strong lift was called the Press. At the age of 16, I could to lift my body weight of 123 pounds. The following year, I was in a different age and weight category and held the record of press and the clean and jerk for a few years. I have the trophy to prove it. Wes went on to become the Olympic track and field coach for the Canadian team at the 1976 Montreal Olympics. I was proud to be part of the crowd for the opening ceremony. Wes also became the weight-lifting coach for the Canadian team in the 1971, 1975 Pan-American, 1968, 1976 and 1980 Olympic and 1974, 1977 World Championship games. In 1981, he was recognized by his peers with award of the National Honour Medal from the International Weightlifting Federation.

John didn't sit still either. He started to coach Wes in the shot put after reading books about track and field. John applied physics to sports, all to do with the efficiency of using the arms, legs and rest of the body in the best way possible. His experience led him to becoming the coach of Harry Jerome. Harry was then world champion in the 100-yard and 100-metre race.

It all goes to show, what you do in your teen years, you end up doing in adulthood.

NEW CANADIAN CLASSES

In 1952, the New Canadian classes were introduced to Strathcona. These were full of newly arrived Chinese from Hong Kong and the classes were the English as a Second Language classes of the day. China had been overtaken by the Communist Party in 1949, so a flood of immigrants and refugees subsequently poured out of Hong Kong. Most students were slightly older than us and spoke little English.

At first there was resentment between the Canadian-born Chinese and the new arrivals. We called them "China Boys" and had snowball fights in the winter on the playground. We teased and taunted them, much to my later regret. After a while, though, we became friends. I became friends with Tom, for example, who lived in a narrow building on Shanghai Alley. He was quite an artist and used to draw Bugs Bunny, Daffy Duck, Porky Pig, and all the other cartoon characters. Another friend was Steve, who was a wizard at photography. Many graduates from the New Canadian Classes eventually became successful business owners.

CHINESE LANGUAGE SCHOOL

Being young in Chinatown meant going to Chinese language school after regular school. It was a drag. I must have attended at least three different schools, and spent at least two years in the same grade, much to the consternation of Father. The first one I attended was on the same block as Father's store. It was held in a temporary room above the Max Goldberg Plumbing shop until the following year when the Chinese Public School called Wah

Kiu, relocated to the Chinese Nationalist Building at the corner of Pender and Gore. The school was on the third floor and as there was no elevator, we had to walk up the stairs.

The teachers were really crabby. They were great believers in discipline and didn't hesitate to use the strap. My friend Sonny believed the teachers had come recently from China and that memories of war were fresh in their minds, so the brand of discipline they imposed was a necessity from their homeland. Like other students, I had my fair share of the strap. It was a bamboo rod with one end smashed into sharp strands. Once the strands slammed into flesh, it was time to scream. The pain was agonising. That was discipline then, but nowadays there are other restraints for that kind of misbehaviour.

Chinese language school started at four in the afternoon, an hour after regular public school finished. There were several schools in Chinatown. The Chinese Freemasons at Pender and Carrall ran the Tai Kong. It was free to members of the Chinese Freemasons. Another was the Mon Keong run by the Wong Family Association on Pender between Columbia and Main. The third was the Wah Kiu which eventually moved again, this time to a former church, kitty-corner from Strathcona School. Every day, I would return home, get a bite to eat, grab my Chinese schoolbooks and bag, and walk to the language school.

If I arrived early, I would play ping-pong with my friends. The girls played mungo sungo. The girls would kick a ball made of shredded newspapers, tied together by a rubber band, like a kind of pompom. The idea was to keep the shredded ball off the ground as long as possible by standing on one leg and kicking from the inside of the heel with the other leg. Once I was sought out by some friends who wanted my pencil drawings. I was fond of sketching warplanes, usually in dogfights. I drew details of the planes, which was appreciated by my audience. Another friend, Wesley, drew horses, and he was also in demand.

In school we learned a little about history and poetry. We practised calligraphy with ink and brushes. Our exercise books contained pages where we slipped a template in between. The template was visible through the paper and we practised copying the written words. In less than two years we switched from ink and brush to ballpoint pens. Ballpoint had just been introduced and though it eliminated the old method, it never replaced the beauty of ink and brush strokes.

Early ballpoint pens were leaky. One year, our class knew ahead of time what the test questions were but which one would we get? In preparation, I wrote some possible answers on the palms of both hands before entering the classroom. Admittedly, it was cheating but believe me, I needed all the help I could get. At test time, I recognized some questions on the paper and opened my hand to write the answers. I had to be careful because the teacher was watching us from the front of the class and occasionally strolled up and down the aisles. When his back was turned, I opened my left palm only to find I couldn't read the answers. I was so sweaty that the ink had smudged, and it was made even worse by my rubbing my wet palm on my pants.

FISH AND CHIPS, ANYBODY?

I attended Chinese language school at the same time I was at Lord Strathcona Elementary School. Every afternoon, when class was over at three, I would go home, chat with Father, pick up my school bag, and head off to Chinese Public School just before four o'clock. This was the daily routine of most of the Chinese kids in Chinatown.

For Jackie Yee it was the same, except he went to a different Chinese school called Mon Keong on Pender Street. Jackie and I hung around together a lot. Both our fathers spoke the same village dialect. In fact, Father enjoyed talking with Jackie in the Loo Doo dialect which I never mastered as well as Jackie did. He lived in the Butler Hotel in the area on Water Street which later became known as Gastown. I'm not too clear about what Jackie's parents did but his father went out of town quite a lot, and though he had brothers, Jackie was often left alone.

One time, Jackie bought a bag of fish and chips one afternoon before going to Chinese school. The only problem with fish and chips was the smell of the oil and vinegar. Nonetheless he was hungry and took a chance in bringing it to class. His classroom was on the mezzanine and he was in the last row overlooking the main floor. When his teacher walked in the room, Jackie quickly flipped open his desktop to hide the fish and chips, but there was nothing he could do about the smell. The teacher immediately demanded to know who it belonged to. No one answered. They were afraid of him because he'd enforce discipline with a bamboo stick. He was fond of whacking one end of the stick till it broke into fine fibres that stung painfully on a student's palm. "All right," he said. "I'm going to examine all the desks one by one and when I do find the troublemaker, I'm going to give him a strapping he won't forget."

Jackie squirmed in his seat and wondered what to do. He hated the teacher and this was probably as good as any time to quit the class. After all, he didn't pay much attention to the lessons and hated school. Halfway through the inspection the teacher turned his back for a minute, and Jackie quickly opened his desk and tossed the small paper bag of fish and chips over his shoulder to the floor below. A yelp shot up. Seconds later, a woman with a wide brimmed hat, covered with chips, stomped into the classroom, "What kind of class are you teaching?" she demanded of the teacher. Wordlessly he stumbled for an explanation and turned in Jackie's direction. But he was already gone.

Postscript: Jackie became a social worker. He was also the first Chinese Canadian elected to the local school board.

Church

I didn't attend much Sunday School, but I was taken by Jennie to the evening sermon on Sundays. It was there at one sermon that the minister revealed a Great Truth. He said that God understood Chinese. I was stunned by this revelation. Though I was brought up with a Chinese background, I was of the opinion that God belonged to the English-speaking world, so for Him to understand Chinese was amazing. This may be the reason why I didn't bother to learn Chinese!

Chinatown, 1950

Dumplings
shrimp, siu mai, potstickers

MINI DONUTS AT THE INTERURBAN DEPOT

A block away from Chinatown at Carrall and Hastings Street was the head office of the old BC Electric company. It was also the main depot for the interurban trams. The interurban trains were fun to travel on. The cars were high up. Being small, I was always given a hand up my Father or the conductor. There were two rows of seats. All the seat covers were rattan. If you were wearing shorts and got up, there would be a waffle iron pattern on your bottom. Women used to complain about their nylons being snagged by the loose wicker.

The tram driver always blew a whistle before stopping at different stations and intersections. In between, the tram went so fast that nearby houses, trees, and mountains flew by. The tram rumbled on overpasses high above busy streets and it was fun to see cars and people looking like small toys. As the tram rumbled on, it would sway from side to side and clack along the tracks.

While waiting on those interurban platforms to board the trams with Father, I developed a fondness for mini donuts. The platform was next to a vendor who had a doughnut machine. I would press my nose against the warm glass plate window and watch a dispenser plunk a doughy ring into the boiling oil. A conveyor belt carried the doughnut through the boiling oil long enough to cook, and dropped it into a basket for cooling at the end. A worker dressed in white would take the doughnuts and dip them into different coloured icing and then sprinkle crushed nuts or tiny candy balls on them.

WO FAT AND BOSTON CREAM PIES

Father took time off during the fall just prior to the Moon Festival to help the bakers at Wo Fat, an old bakery on Pender Street. The men from the bakery and my father were from the same village. They greeted each other as old friends, and whenever they met, caught up with news from China. The bakery did not display all its wares in the windows. It was as if everyone in Chinatown knew what was being offered, and many regular customers knew that. They made tasty sponge cake, almond cookies, and cookies in the shape of a Buddha but, best of all, their famous moon cakes. Those were made once a year. They were round, about 3 to 4 centimetres thick, and stuffed with black bean paste, diced almonds, half a salted egg yolk, sesame seeds, etc. They were so rich that it was a challenge just to eat the whole cake at one sitting.

I also liked eating other baked goods too. The BC Royal Café on Pender Street served the best Boston cream pies in town. No kidding. The pie consisted of two layers of sponge cake separated by a thick filling of custard and topped off with whipped cream, real whipped cream. I ate the same kind of pies at other restaurants on Granville Street such as Scott's and the Sky Dinner, but they were never as good as the ones at the BC Royal. They also had cream puffs, babyfingers, butterhorns and honey twists. A customer could sit down at the counter, order a pastry and a cup of coffee, which was customarily served with dollops of sugar and cream, whether you wanted them or not.

First Chinese Drive-In Restaurant

In 1954, an enterprising Chinese named Joe Quan opened the first Chinese food drive-in in Canada. He picked a spot where a gas station had once stood on Pender Street, and pulled in enough business that he opened an outlet in the suburbs. Later, when I was working as a columnist for the *Chinatown News,* I asked what his best seller was. Was it chow mein? Sweet and sour spareribs? He took me aside and swore me to secrecy: it was fish and chips.

Lee's Confectionery

Most evenings after dinner, Father would do the dishes, sweep the floor, and leave the store just as F.P. arrived. He left so that he could help George Lee out at the confectionery store on Hastings Street. The two men not only came from the same village, but also were active in the district associations. These were organised by people who came from the same area or district in China. Their purpose was to help each other out in looking for a job, a place to live, and sometimes to lend money to those in need. They also arranged for transportation of remains back to China. In the late nineteenth and early twentieth centuries, the Chinese were discriminated against in a society which clearly did not welcome them. So strong was this feeling of not belonging that many Chinese wished to be buried in their home villages. It became a ritual every seven years to dig up remains, clean the bones, place them in small wooden boxes, and store them in a warehouse at the Chinese cemetery in Victoria to await shipment to China.

Father enjoyed helping George at the store. George and his family lived at the back of the store. He was married to Lillian who hosted a mahjong circle every night at the back of the store. They were quite a couple; George was tall and lean and Lillian was short and stout. They had three daughters: Irene, Bessie, and Eva. Bessie was the same age as I was. Even though Mrs. Lee fed me her special corn fritters or steamed chicken, more often than not, I visited their store because the Lees sold comic books. I would sit at the racks going through all the comic books while Father and George discussed politics, the ladies played mahjong, and Bessie practised "Heart and Soul" on the piano. Sometimes I got thirsty and helped myself to a bottle of Coke from the Coca-Cola cooler.

It was also at this time I learned about sex, well, maybe not learned but peeked at the differences. On the racks was a nudist club magazine and when no one was looking, I sneaked a forbidden look at the contents. I was fascinated by the images of nude women, but was always puzzled why the women were missing a penis. I thought at first it had been airbrushed out but that wasn't possible as the men certainly showed their organs. I just couldn't understand. Sex was a subject Father never discussed with me.

One day in 1948, George Lee bought a gleaming new black, four-door Chevrolet. Father was impressed; after all, how many Chinese had their own cars? George was quite proud of his car and often invited us for drives, once to Boundary Bay to dig for clams, and another time, a big favourite, to the White Spot drive-in on Granville Street in the Marpole area. At that time, a drive to Marpole was like a drive in the country. We sat in the car as the carhop took our orders and returned with long sliding trays that hooked on the inside of the windows. It was such a novelty to eat fried chicken and chips sitting in the car. Boundary Bay was fun, too. That was where we went digging for clams. The beach was long and wide at low tide, perfect for searching for telltale holes in the wet sand where the clams were. Once they were spotted we had to dig quickly, otherwise the clams would escape.

EARLIEST MEMORIES AND BLACKOUTS

My earliest recollection in my first three years was when F.P. took me to Powell Street and we entered the most beautiful building. It had large display windows and the exterior walls were covered with beautiful black marble tiles. Inside the Maikawa Department Store were men's and women's clothing, but the most exciting things for me were the various toys. Woodward's on Hastings

Early morning in Chinatown circa the 1950s

was much larger, of course, but Maikawa stood out for me. Little did I realize that weeks later Japan Town would no longer exist.

I remember the sound of air raid sirens wailing in the evening. The bombing of Pearl Harbor brought fear to the west coast and the realization that a Japanese attack on Vancouver was very possible. The government built gun turrets facing the sea at Point Grey at UBC and at Ferguson Point in Stanley Park.

When the sirens wailed Father quickly pulled down the blinds on the front windows and door of the shop and turned off all lights. My eldest brother lit a candle and we sat in the dark, waiting for the all-clear signal. It was frightening because I didn't know what it was about. All I knew was that danger, whether real or not, was close by. My brother made it scarier by holding the candle under his chin and casting strange and grotesque shadows on his face, all the while making eerie noises.

The blackouts weren't the only thing that frightened me. There were the programs on the radio, which my brothers and sister listened to. The radio, about the size of a basketball, was perched on top of a kitchen cabinet. Radio dramas in those days used a lot of sound effects and if you huddled in the dark, as we did, you could imagine the story. Popular programs such as "The Shadow," "The Mysterious Traveller," and "Suspense" had all the elements of drama and mystery: listening to the dialogue and sound effects frightened us and gave us chills running down our spines.

THE JAPANESE AND THE EVACUATION

My brother told me that a Japanese family lived in the store next to us. He said they were friendly people but after the bombing of Pearl Harbor, all Japanese citizens in Vancouver were looked upon with suspicion both inside and outside of Chinatown. According to my brother, he woke up one morning, and found our neighbours gone. Father told him that all the Japanese people had probably been taken away by the RCMP in the middle of the night.

Wah went to school that morning and the first thing he noticed were empty desks where Japanese students had sat. There was a tremendous feeling of shock and loss among the teachers and students. They cried over the empty desks. Nothing like this had ever happened before.

That spring of 1942 I stood next to F.P., holding his hand, on the overpass overlooking the railway platforms at the CPR railway station. Below us were long dark lines of people silently boarding the trains. Their destinations were the internment camps in the interior of BC and beyond. The Japanese had been forced out of their homes and businesses on Powell Street. Like Chinatown, Japan Town had been a busy and bustling community, full of shops where you could buy tasty fishcake at Kay's Fish Market, get a haircut, or eat sukiyaki.

The government's orders were to evacuate those of Japanese origin at least a hundred miles from the coast. The sky was a dull grey and rain pelted us that day. F.P. and I watched the trains. I held his hand tightly. There was sadness in his eyes. The place where we stood had unpleasant memories for him. He turned around to face a nearby dingy brick building. It was on the other side of the railway yard sitting on the waterfront at the foot of Thurlow Street – it was the Immigration building, a dreaded place. For years when the Chinese first arrived by steamers they were escorted to that building for questioning and paid their $500 head tax. If deemed necessary, they were detained in cells for days or weeks. It was an experience not often recounted.

When the last of the Japanese were gone, their properties were eventually sold at giveaway prices. In their wake, residents of Chinatown wore homemade badges on their lapels, declaring themselves as Chinese and not Japanese. They wanted to make it clear to the world that we were not Japanese.

THE CHINESE PENDER Y

In Chinatown there was no such thing as a community centre. Any social events or activities were held in church halls or family or benevolent associations' meeting halls, so the Vancouver YWCA opened a Chinatown branch on Pender Street, steps away from Gore Avenue, sometime in the early 1940s. It was located in a small narrow building used as housing. The Y was actually a storefront, long and narrow, but it served its purpose. The Chinese Y, as it was later known, was open to both boys and girls. Wah and Jennie attended the Y as it was a place for a social get together after school, particularly when there were dances on Valentine's Day. My sister, in particular, enjoyed meeting her friends there and was involved with a theatrical group called The Moongate Players.

They fundraised by putting on stage plays and even travelled to Victoria and Seattle.

In 1946 I joined the Mount Everest Troop Number 32 Cubs. For the first few weeks, I learned how to make fire using two pieces of stick and how to tell directions from looking at the moss on trees and read the stars at night for the time. Every evening when we gathered, we went through a ritual of gathering in a circle and squatting, pretending to be wolves, holding our fingers to the side of our faces as ears and making a howling sound. It was fun being a cub. Among other highlights, we went on a hiking trip to Lynn Valley and helped collecting money in Chinatown for a charity.

In 1953, the Y moved up the street to Dunlevy Street, across from the Chinese United Church. It was there that I joined the Dragon Club. It was for young teens who met every Friday night at eight. The Dragon Club was led by a young architect named David Molson. By 1953, we were going into different high schools and the only way we could get together was through the Y. Some of us attended Britannia High, others Vancouver Tech, and still others King Edward High. The Y was an ideal place for us to continue our friendships. It was the same thing for the girls; they also met on Friday, and their club was called the Y'ettes. It was a nice arrangement, particularly for planning for social events such as dances. Some members of the Dragons were also in a basketball team sponsored by a well-known restaurant and did very well.

The Social Clubs

One Sunday, when I was about eleven years old, Father had to look for someone. He had no choice but to take me along so we went to the social club, which was really a gambling den. To get into the club from Pender Street, you had to pay a fee at the front wicket. Father explained to the clerk that he was looking for so-and-so inside. The clerk looked at my father, then at me, shrugged his shoulders, and nodded his head toward the door. He must have thought, how many men would take a kid into a gambling den? He must be looking for someone who owes him money.

We went inside a large room and all I could see were different tables with men sitting or standing by. The air was smoky as everyone in those days smoked a lot; along one wall, I saw several old men sitting around a bucket. They were passing a metal pipe, one end being in the bucket, and smoking the other end. I heard men slam their mahjong tiles hard on the table and swear. There were bursts of laughter and loud talking.

Finally Father saw his friend, who had just finished playing a round of mahjong. The friend looked over, smiled, and came to talk to Father. They chatted for a while as I stood restlessly next to Father. Then the man bent down and said, "Your son? What a nice boy." With that, he pulled out a wallet, gave Father some money, turned to me, and gave me a crisp ten dollar bill. I stood there, stunned, not saying a word. Father poked me in the back, "What do you say, son?" I stammered a thank you and the two men laughed. They said goodbye to each other and Father and I left the room. Out on the street, I took a breath of fresh air, grateful to leave the smoke filled room. Father must have felt the same way too. Immediately he took me by the hand and we entered the BC Royal Café, sat down, and ordered a butterhorn for each of us.

BANQUETS

Once a year, our district association held a big banquet. It was also a time to renew memberships and to visit with old friends. The day would begin in the meeting hall at 260 East Pender Street. All the men and their wives and children were there. There was a happy atmosphere, everyone seemed genuinely pleased to see each other and of course, the treasurer was happy as he collected the annual membership dues. He sat at a roll-top desk, writing off receipts with a fountain pen while an assistant took down names and wrote with Chinese ink and brush the person's name, dues, name of the home village, and the date on bright red coloured ribbons. The ribbons were then hung proudly on a large bulletin board for all to see. Later in the afternoon while the day was still bright, a photographer with a studio camera on a tripod stood in the middle of the street as most of the members posed for a group photograph in front of the association building.

Father particularly enjoyed the gathering. It was a time for him to relax and catch up with the news from his fellow villagers. He really looked forward to the banquets.

I didn't. I thought they were boring.

They were usually held at the W.K. Gardens, a popular restaurant on the second floor of a building in Chinatown. On weeknights, the restaurant was a place to dine and dance, usually with a live band. It was a popular place and the food was always good. At banquet time, all the tables were filled and extra tables were set up on the dance floor. A bottle of Johnny Walker Red Label was set on each table, compliments of the association. There were also bottles of soft drinks for kids like me. The food was too fancy for my tastes. Father, on the other hand, relished the gourmet dishes. In fact, I used to hate the Chinese black mush-rooms, but I loved the abalone. There was also rock cod done up in deep-fried batter and covered with tomato sauce.

I used to squirm at those functions. It was easy for me to become restless. For some reason, none of the other adults brought their children and I ended up being about the only youngster at the table, but then again I didn't realize Chinatown was almost a bachelors' society. After while I found out that Father was an executive, the loan officer of the association, and being in that post, that he had to sit with the rest of the executive. Unlike my father, they were less fortunate, being without their wives and families because of the Chinese Exclusion Act.

Once, as the adults at my table were conversing in Chinese, I complained loudly that no one spoke English. Without skipping a beat, one elderly gentleman turned to me and said, "And what would you like to talk about?" My face turned a hot red, and I was ready to crawl under my seat and stay there. I have since learned never to judge before learning all the facts.

Zhongshan Association annual photo, taken on Gore Avenue
Larry and Father in the front row, four from the left

Savoury
chicken feet, turnip cake, tripe

Spoil the Child and Spare the Rod

I don't think Father ever heard that expression, "spoil the child and spare the rod." Whenever I was in trouble with him, he would grab a yardstick and without hesitation would whack my legs while screaming and yelling at me. He would go on for what seemed like hours. Looking back now, he was probably applying the same discipline as his father did to him. Father had a short temper, but once he blew it off, he was back to his normal self. One day, as he was hitting my legs with the yardstick, I stood up to him by grabbing the yardstick away. He was surprised and stopped shouting at me. We were both quiet, and he never again raised that yardstick at me, but he sure kept yelling at me!

After, on the odd occasion, Father and I would have our disagreements. There were two that I remembered, and both had to do with clocks. Father had an alarm clock, one with a large face and two bells on top. That day, I found a small screwdriver and started to take the clock apart. I was curious to see how the clock worked and how the alarm went off. However, once I had the pieces apart, I realized that I would have to put the pieces back together. I was confused and hopeless. That was when Father came along, saw the clock in many pieces on the table, and screamed at me.

Father had by his bedside a beautiful European clock encased in glass so you can see the inner workings, the springs, gears, and rotating vanes. Curious once again, I pulled out the screwdriver. Pulling apart the clock was difficult as it was very well made piece, but I persisted and succeeded but again, I couldn't remember how the individual pieces went together. I think I must have really angered Father. I guess it was an expensive clock. Not only did he scream and shout at me, he physically picked me up by my neck and pants, carried me out of the store, and threw me onto the sidewalk!

Another time, I was so upset, I sulked after another scolding and walked out the back of the store with Father still shouting after me. I didn't go very far. Our backyard was really a parking lot for the other stores so I hid from sight behind a car when Father came out looking for me. When it was close to dinnertime and he came out again, I revealed myself and together we walked silently back to the store.

Larry in front of Father's store on Main Street

THE DAY A CAR RAN ME OVER

I think I was eight years old. It was one of those warm summer evenings when, after dinnertime, Father was still at work at the sewing machine and I decided to go and visit a friend. When I got there, we played for a while until I decided to return home. The evening was still bright and I walked north along Main Street until I reached the corner of Pender. Home was half a block away. I stopped, watching the red light until it turned green. As it did, I stepped off the curb and suddenly, from my left side, a Model T-Ford struck me in the leg. Taken by surprise, my body twisted and I collapsed with both hands onto the pavement. I remember looking up at the underbelly of the car. There was the long axis, the wirings, the transmission, all there as the car passed over me. The car screeched to a stop just in front of me. I was lying prone, right between the wheels. The driver, a Chinese man, rushed out and asked if I was all right.

I got up, a bit shaky. My nose started to bleed. The driver quickly gave me a handkerchief. "Are you all right?" he asked again. I nodded. I couldn't really speak. I cleared my throat. I croaked, "Yes, I'm okay," as I brushed myself off. A crowd started to gather but seeing that I wasn't seriously hurt, they drifted away. "I'm sorry," said the driver. "I didn't see you." I offered the blood-soaked handkerchief to him. "No, no," he said, "Keep it. Your nose is still bleeding." He got back into his car and drove off. I recognized the car. It was used as a vegetable delivery truck for the people living in Strathcona, the area east of Chinatown.

The excitement over, I continued on my way home. As I closed the front door behind me and walked through the empty store to the rear, I could see Father hunched over the sewing machine, working on an order of shirts. I sauntered through the curtained entrance to our living quarters, passing him. He called me but luckily didn't look up. My nose had stopped bleeding but if he had known I had been run over by a car, he would have killed me right there!

SATURDAY MATINEE MOVIES

Growing up in Chinatown in the 1950s meant there was no role model for me. There were no Asian actors such as Bruce Lee, Jackie Chan, or Jet Li then. All we had were Caucasian actors dressed as Chinese in Charlie Chan's movies. There was even a Chinese-American actor named Richard Loo who played a Japanese pilot in World War Two movies and spouted lines like "Die, Yankee Dog, die" as he nose-dived his Zero plane towards an American plane. I grew up on a diet of Saturday matinees filled with Hopalong Cassidy, Gene Autry and Roy Rogers. They weren't exactly men with whom I could identify.

On Saturdays, my friend Jack Say Yee, who lived in a hotel owned by his father in what is now called Gastown, called for me at the store to go to Saturday matinees. Both our fathers came from the same village, which was how I got to know Jack and his brothers. We had a choice of theatres near Chinatown. On Main Street, half a block from our store, was the Star Theatre, right next to the police station. It was an old auditorium where the floor creaked with every footstep. There was also the Beacon Theatre and the Rex Theatre across from each other on Hastings just off Carrall Street.

The Beacon was a grand-looking 1930s theatre once known as the Pantages, built of marble on the outside and with a stage large enough for live performances. Once, I saw elephants perform on the stage between movies. The theatres in those days did a lot of things to attract customers.

The Rex had a steep sloping floor with a mezzanine separating the upper and lower floors. I liked the Rex, as it showed a lot of my favourite movies. I also liked keeping an eye on the illuminated clock near the screen. On the face was "Bulova," with the name of the jewellery store circling the clock. I didn't realize it then but years later my friends said that Chinese patrons were segregated in one section of the theatre. Thinking back, I do remember that there was always an usher at the entrance who always led me to the left side of the upper floor.

Our all-time favourite was the Lux. For twelve cents admission, we saw a double bill of westerns and three cartoons. We followed the adventures of Roy Rogers, Gene Autry, Hopalong Cassidy, Durango Kid, and Buster Crabbe. We enjoyed the antics of the Bowery Boys, a group of friends living in Brooklyn. The characters were played by Leo Gorcey as Slip Mahoney and Huntz Hall as Sach, who always seemed to get into trouble or get picked on because they were poor but who managed in the end to save the situation. They were a group we identified with a great deal. The movie characters came from the east side and we were from the east side. They were poor and we were poor. They were the underdogs and so were we. In the early 1950s, movies from Hong Kong made it to Vancouver, and the Lux Theatre on East Hastings Street was the place to go. The movies were in black and white, and occasionally, one could see oil blotches or spots on the screen. One film looked as if someone had spilt cooking oil on it. Maybe it was poor quality celluloid.

My father's favourites were movies whose characters flew through the air. You could see the wires from actors' bodies or sometimes a rear screen projection. He loved the action films, as it was such an escape from everyday boredom. Besides, the theatre sold hot dogs in the lobby. Father thought this was a great idea and never failed to buy one.

After the movies, Jack and I would walk over to radio station CKWX on Seymour Street in time to take part in a radio program. A moving van company sponsored a program called "The Crone Safety Show" hosted by Bob Hutton. There was always a full audience because the host would pick someone at random to come up to the stage to answer a question. If the answer was correct, there was a cash prize. The catch was that the prize was determined by throwing a ring at a board that had different amounts. Jack and I were lucky enough to be called up and often walked away with money in our pockets, often enough for a couple of weeks of movies!

Left Alone

Wah graduated from UBC and left home in 1949 for Seattle to attend the University of Washington. He would be working toward a Masters degree in political science. The next year, Jennie left home for Ontario. As a young woman growing up in a predominantly male home, she was frustrated without Mother to guide her through womanhood. As Father didn't want to lose any more of his family members, he was dominating and controlling. Jennie, unable to cope with his overbearing manners, decided it was time for her to leave home. She considered Chinatown a village where she was stifled and unappreciated. She dated white boys, but when my father found out, he literally hit the roof. Looking back, I can see now why he wouldn't want to lose his only daughter to a lo fan. I remember one night when Jennie came home late from a date but Father wouldn't let her in the house. He was in a rage, screaming at her until she cried, asking for forgiveness.

So I was left alone with Father. It wasn't bad except that whenever I was in a school play or other activities, there were no family members to cheer me on. They missed my growing up years. Some of my friends felt that I was being a patsy by being left behind to look after my aging father, but that wasn't the case. He was very active even after his retirement and doted on his grandchildren from his paper daughter, but that is another story.

He was accommodating. As a shirt tailor, he made shirts my size and in the colours I wanted. One day, I was thinking out loud how nice it would be if I had a real belt with a gun holster to play cowboys. He made what I wanted from a piece of leatherette. I was the only one among my friends who had a real gun holster and belt. On the other hand, just before Christmas, I was flipping through a Lionel train catalogue, staring at pictures of trains with real smoke coming out of stacks. Father knew I wanted a set, but all he could afford was a wind-up train on a small track.

Another time, a friend of Father's left a movie projector behind. It was a Bell and Howell with a hand crank to keep the reels going. There was a plug for the electric light bulb and lenses to project the images and, of course, there was no sound. It was easy to thread the film from the top reel through the guide behind the lens and to the receiving reel. I had 16 mm films of Tom Mix, Charlie Chaplin, and Hopalong Cassidy. The films were from a company called Castle Films. I made a small movie screen out of a silver covered shoebox and even painted a black frame to look realistic. One of my friends who was really fascinated by the movie projector was Sonny Choy. He laughed when I cranked reels backwards to see a cowboy leaping off away from his horse or a posse riding backwards, distancing themselves from the bad guys. The reels only lasted five minutes, but the projector was the best toy I ever had.

THE ONE-EYED MONSTER

Life in Chinatown was simple. For one thing, there was no television, at least not until 1953 when Hoy's Electronics and Appliances on the corner introduced the first television set in Chinatown. People were excited and they pointed to the window, "Hey look, television."

The television set was mounted inside the front window and there was a small speaker on the outside so that all passersby could see and hear the program beaming in from Seattle. The picture, white and blue colour with lots of interweaving lines, was barely recognizable, while the sound, travelling some 150 miles north, was fuzzy. Hoy was the first to install a tall rooftop antenna pointing south to Seattle, a preview of what would become commonplace in the coming years. Hoy had the television tuned in to KING-TV, the first and only station at that time. It was exciting to see movies, game shows, and the news, especially the latter. The Korean War was on and the daily news often showed the latest air battles over Korea. The pictures were from the gun camera of an American jet in a dogfight with an enemy plane. It was fascinating to see the actual footage.

One day, Fred, who lived on Georgia Street, invited me to his house to watch television. His parents had bought a new set. When I arrived, we all sat in the dark in the living room. Television was such a novelty then, we watched all the commercials and programs, whether they were good or bad. A soft halo of light surrounded the screen; apparently it was designed to ease eyestrain. I guess that was how early television came to be known as the one-eyed monster. I was really glad that a friend had a television set. I was tired of watching Hoy's television from the street. Most programs I heard on the radio became television shows such as the Red Skelton Show, Ozzie and Harriet, the Jack Benny Show, and the Lone Ranger.

One day, shortly after CBC-TV opened in 1953 on Georgia and Bute, I heard that their reception room was open in the evenings. The studio was quite a distance from Chinatown but I was curious and after dinner one Sunday evening, I walked through Chinatown, crossed the Georgia Viaduct, made my way through downtown, and strolled straight along Georgia Street until I reached the studios on Bute Street.

A commissionaire was on duty and I politely asked to watch television. He looked at me, smiled, and said that I could go in and watch the Ed Sullivan show, which had started a few minutes earlier. I rushed into the room to find several other people there, who like me, had come out of curiosity. We smiled at each other and settled down to watch. For one summer, I made a ritual of walking every Sunday evening to the CBC studios from Chinatown just to watch Ed Sullivan.

HALLOWEEN AND THE FIRECRACKER WARS

I swear that the Chinese community in the fifties just didn't catch on to Halloween. I suppose it was incomprehensible to the community because of the strange custom of dressing in costumes and going door-to-door asking for tricks or treats. The only children who dressed up for Halloween were small, usually carried by their parents. Then there were the teenagers. They didn't bother to dress

Pender Street, 1950

for the occasion or even wear masks. They gathered in groups of four or five and went door to door with bags asking for candies.

Later in the evening, in the heart of Chinatown, these same groups of teens congregated on either side of the street. There would be an air of tension, a feeling that something exciting was going to happen. Some guys would light small packets of small firecrackers, and throw a string of them to the other side. Firecrackers came in all shapes and sizes, including skyrockets, Roman candles, volcanoes, wheels, sparklers, canons, comets and other fireworks now banned.

The firecrackers would pop and bang and echo against buildings. The noise added to the spectacle as the colours of flares bloomed over Chinatown. Gradually, larger fireworks joined the exchange until Roman candles and skyrockets whistled and blazed into the sky forcing everyone to look up with amazement. The cloud of thick acrid smoke meant that the crowds couldn't see each other across the street. Few elderly Chinese dared to venture out, preferring to peek from behind their windows and shake their heads.

When smoky haze finally lifted, masses of shredded red paper were revealed all over the pavement, and the crowd thinned. Occasionally a couple of teens had minor burns to the faces and perhaps had a fingertip or two blown off, but nothing more serious happened. Surprisingly, the police were never called and no serious fights broke out. There was little car traffic on Pender Street; perhaps there were warning signs to the drivers to avoid Chinatown for a while. Just as quickly as the fireworks began, the crowd disappeared, and the streets were once again quiet.

THE SWAMPS OF FALSE CREEK FLATS

Near Strathcona School and the railway tracks was a large bushy area. In Vancouver's early days, the body of water called False Creek came up past Main Street. Eventually the land was drained and became swampy. During the 1930s depression, homeless people camped out on the flats and also did so after World War Two. By then, the grounds were covered with bushes and once in the early fifties, our science class made a day trip there to catch tadpoles in glass jars.

We called it the False Creek Flats. One summer, John and I tramped through the thistle jungle and immediately started to perspire. It seems that the field of thistles trapped the heat from the sun, which was unbearable. The thistles were above our heads and thick: John and I had a wooden pole to beat down a path so we could see where we were going. We had to watch for the sharp prickly thorns, and at times had our arms scratched or parts of the plants sticking to our clothes. We whacked our way to the Grandview Cut, a gully carved out for a single railway track to connect the rail yards near Main Street with points east and south. We entered the gully and walked along the tracks, immediately feeling the cool air. As we walked I suddenly dropped to my knees and bent my ear to a rail.

"What the heck are you doing?"

"Shhh," I said. "I'm listening to hear if any trains are coming."

John laughed. "Where did you get that idea?"

"Watching cowboy movies. You know. The Indians always listen to the track for the trains."

John laughed again. "There's another way."

"Yeah? What?"

He pointed to a signal light by the track. It was green on one side and red on the other. "See the red? It means you can't go this way but see the green? It means the track is clear to go this way." Just like a traffic light.

HUCKLEBERRY FINN

As young boys, we were usually doing something interesting when we weren't in school. We were always on the lookout for cops patrolling the streets. One day, Farmer was selling squabs when he saw a cop approaching. The squabs were in a carton but there was no place to hide it. He scooped up the squabs and stuffed them under his shirt, zipped up his jacket, and walked past the cop with an uncontrollable smile, not because he was getting away with it, but because the squabs were tickling him. Though usually, it was a man we called the Pigeon King who sold squabs on the streets of Chinatown. He was an old Irishman, redheaded, unshaven, his suit jacket and pants wrinkled and filthy. Not to mention smelly. He would snatch baby pigeons from their nests underneath the old Georgia Viaduct, shove them in a gunnysack, and sell them on Pender Street.

One day, we read the book *Huckleberry Finn* in school and when a group of us were walking down the street from school and Farmer said, "Hey, you guys. You know what? We can build a raft, just like in Huckleberry Finn."

"Oh sure, Farmer," we said. "And go where?"

"Across the Burrard Inlet."

The more we thought about it, the more enthusiastic we were. We were fairly familiar with Burrard Inlet. We fished off Ballentyne pier with a simple nylon line, lead, hooks, and worms. We caught mostly bullheads, and always pulled up pieces of rubber tires, kelp, and tin cans. There was nothing to take home but we had fun.

So why couldn't we built a raft and sail to North Vancouver? Farmer said that all we needed was some driftwood logs and to lash them together. "Hey, there's all kind of driftwood. They could be telephone poles, small tree trunks, anything." I should mention that in school at this time, we were a year or two away from taking Industrial Arts so we really had no experience with hammer and nails. We went to a small beach by the cannery but the logs we found were too large. After all, we were only twelve and could only manage so much.

We made two attempts. The first was a crude effort with small driftwoods tied together with twine. We nailed some planks cross-wise which at least gave the raft a half decent appearance. It was ready to launch. Ivan Sam volunteered to test it out. He stood on the raft with a pole while we pushed it off, but that didn't help at all. Finally Farmer rolled his pant legs up and entered the water to push the raft away. He cursed and groaned but finally it was free and floating. We let out a big cheer.

The raft had drifted a few feet from the beach when Skippy, Ivan's dog, decided to join his master. Skippy leapt into the water, paddled to Ivan, and tried to climb aboard while Ivan frantically yelled, "Get off, Skippy, get off. You're tipping the raft." Skippy managed to clamber aboard but when the twine and the nails started to come apart, he jumped off and swam to shore, leaving Ivan to slip off a log into Burrard Inlet.

On the second attempt, we found a large pallet, which we thought was a natural raft. This time, John volunteered and as the rest of us pushed the raft off, water seeped through the planks and John courageously made a smart salute, saying, "Boys, I'm going down with the ship" as he sank into the waters…up to his knees.

JUNKING

A group of us went junking. It was a 1950s style of recycling. We visited the few deserted houses on Pender Street, destined for demolition. By the time we arrived most of them already had had a head start from the demolition company. What we did was meet at John's house. I brought my little wagon but unfortunately it wasn't a very good one. The wheels were wooden, and in time, they wore out so the wagon tended to slow down.

We entered the houses at night using flashlights since the power was cut off. We would rip out the electrical wiring, which was easy to do, and take away copper and brass pipes, as much as the wagon could carry. We would then leave and return to John's house to stash our collection. The next day we would burn the cotton insulation off the copper wires and bundle them for the trip to the junk dealer. He usually gave us a fair price for the bare copper wire and the plumbing fixtures. He didn't ask where we got the wire and we didn't tell him.

The biggest job we had was the old elementary school called Central High near the Vancouver Sun Tower. It was being torn down for a parking lot. There were four of us, John, Farmer, Wesley, me, and my trusty wagon. We crossed the Georgia Viaduct over False Creek and went along Beatty Street to where the partially demolished school stood. As it was already dark, we began by pulling at the copper wires, ripping them off the ceilings, the walls, wherever they were installed; we were soon covered in dust and plaster.

We gathered enough to load up the wagon. It took all of us to push wires and cram as much as we could into it. With much struggle, we slowly left the building to return by the same route as we had come. Halfway across the viaduct, a police car came by, and I thought, "Oh, oh, now we've had it." We were four boys pulling a small wagon piled with wires. Maybe we looked innocent, maybe the police didn't notice, but they drove past us without stopping.

Another time, we wanted lead pipes. They were commonly used on rooftops to provide ventilation. We were certain that virgin territory existed for lead pipes. Someone came up with an idea, a really brilliant idea. We all agreed and felt we could do the job. It was a daring plan. We were to climb to the rooftops of Chinatown.

One night we slipped down the back alleys carrying empty burlap bags and selected a tall building. We found a couple of wooden crates to stand on as we hoisted ourselves up to the lower rung of a fire escape ladder. We went to the second floor landing where iron stairs took us to a third floor balcony until we reached the fourth floor balcony and again climbed a ladder to the rooftop. It took awhile for our eyes to adjust to the darkness, but finally we made out the lead pipes on the gravel and asphalt roof. We walked slowly and quietly to them.

Since lead pipes are soft and easily sliced with a pocket-knife, it wasn't difficult work to get them. Soon our burlap bag started to bulge and occasionally we could hear sound from the rooms below. Wes was curious and bent over to peer into a pipe. Suddenly, he jerked back and let out a small scream. We looked up and asked what had happened.

"I just saw an eye looking up," he said.

Oh shit, we thought. Better get the hell out before the cops come. We were certain someone would call the police. For some reason, we continued working until we collected all the pipes, shoved them into a burlap sack, and edged our way back down to the fire escape ladder to the ground. As they would say in the novels, we then melted into the shadows.

KOOL-AID

One hot summer in the early fifties, some friends and I visited Wes in his apartment. His parents were away for the day and we decided that we would make Kool-Aid, a popular drink made from flavoured powder, usually orange or cherry, mixed with cold water. We made a big pitcher and relaxed in the living room, feeling the warm breeze and sunshine from the window, sipping the drink.

"Hey you guys," said Farmer. "Let's spice up the Kool-Aid." We all looked at him.

"Yeah," he said, "let's get some mix. I'll go home and get my old man's vodka."

Ivan Sam piped in, "Good idea. Why don't each of us go home and bring a bottle from home?"

So we all left and within an hour returned with our contributions of beer, whiskey, vodka, wine, and gin. We searched for a large pot in Wes's kitchen and poured the mixture of liquor into the Kool-Aid. The resulting brew had a curious taste but was palatable. We added some lemons and ice cubes. At times, the liquor came through with the Kool-Aid feebly touching the palate. We spent the rest of the afternoon drinking and occasionally adding a little more to the brew. Although we didn't get sick or drunk, we did frequent the bathroom more often than usual. I believe that was the last time we drank Kool-Aid.

WET WEEKEND AT LONG BEACH

I met Solomon through a mutual friend who was a student at the Vancouver Art School. At the time, I was in my first year at UBC, and through Paddy, I met many art students who became friends. I was with a group of them when the Peking Chinese Opera Company performed for the first time in Canada in 1960.

Solomon was a social worker in New Westminster and often drove into town to visit me in Chinatown. His father was the Reverend C.C. Shiu who served at Christ Church of China on Keefer Street. Reverend Shiu was one of the few Chinese who came to Canada after 1923, the infamous year when it excluded Chinese from the country. His siblings were all named after Old Testament figures: Daniel, David, Samuel, Esther, Joseph, Joshua, and Elizabeth. They, in turn, named their children after figures from the New Testament.

"How did your father get into Canada?" I asked.

"There were exceptions to the Chinese Exclusion Act. They let him in because he was a minister. He came from China in 1924 to convert Chinese to Christianity. He went to Methodist churches in Saskatchewan, Winnipeg, Hamilton, Montreal, Nanaimo, and finally here. He was in Victoria, too, and that was where he met Mother."

Solomon's mother, Julia, was one of many young women who lived in the Chinese Rescue Home, a place for young girls who had either been abandoned by their parents or orphaned. The home was run by missionaries, who schooled the girls in Christian education and vocational skills.

The Shiu family home was an old turn-of-the-century house with a large living room and dining room on the ground floor and bedrooms upstairs. The kitchen was small, but Mrs. Shiu cooked wonderful and delicious meals there. Solomon often invited me over for dinner without telling his mother, but I was always welcomed, and the Shius became part of an extended family. Mrs. Shiu was a tiny woman, but her heart was big. I often wonder how she managed with such a large family. Solomon always invited me to join in their Easter, Thanksgiving, and Christmas celebrations. We stood around the piano singing songs and, of course, the good reverend blessed our meals. I was always grateful for the warm welcome and closeness of the family gathering as most of my own family lived elsewhere.

One day, Reverend Shiu came to the store and introduced himself to Father. They talked about their sons and how well they got along together. A couple of years later, Reverent Shiu officiated at Father's funeral. It was fitting, I thought, for someone who knew Father personally to do the ceremony.

One long weekend, Solomon and I decided to go to Long Beach on the west coast of Vancouver Island. In addition to his camping gear, he bought a frozen Cornish hen, dry soup, fruits, cookies, and other snacks. We left Vancouver for the Vancouver Island ferry when it was sunny, but by the time we reached Port Alberni, it was raining. At Long Beach, we drove up and down the highway trying to find parking. The whole highway along the length of the beach was crowded and parking was at a premium. Even the beach was crowded but we finally found a space and I parked my Volkswagen Beetle where the sand was dry. We didn't dare park on the damp sand as we knew it was a tidal area. We quickly unpacked the car and pitched the tent on the beach joining many other campers; most of them were cooking over their propane stoves. Luckily our tent was up just as it started to rain. We ducked inside and waited. The rain became a downpour. Sol had intended to cook the Cornish hen on his propane stove outside but instead we settled down to eat cookies and fruits.

The next morning was no better so we decided to leave. We waited for a break in the weather and when it came, quickly took down the tent and packed our gear inside the car. I started it but the rear wheels just spun in the wet sand. Solomon jumped out and tried to push, but we needed something solid for the wheels to take hold so in the pelting rain Solomon and I took turns pushing the car. I tried shifting gears to rock the Beetle back and forth but with no luck. We couldn't find anything to provide traction to the wheels but fortunately a couple of husky men came and pushed us out of the mud. Both of us were soaking wet and cold. We took off our windbreakers, shirts, undershirt, jeans, socks, and shoes, all soaked and clammy, and put on our dry clothing. Unfortunately, moving in and out of the car pushed it deeper into the wet sand. Again, we got out in the rain and pushed. For the second time we were soaked. The wind blew large droplets into the car and I literally had to bail out water from the floor with a coffee cup. It was cold so I turned the heater on.

When we finally got out of the beach, we continued down the highway looking for a motel, which was almost next to impossible on a long weekend, but we did eventually find one. The first thing I asked at the registration desk was whether they had a laundry room. They did, so we checked into our room and pulled off our wet clothing. In the laundry room, we loaded the dryer and reluctantly stripped down to our undershorts. There we sat in the laundry room, two nearly nude men, crossing our arms over our laps when other guests came in to use the washing machines. We tried not to stare at each other to keep from giggling, or worse, laughing hysterically.

Barbeque ducks on display in Chinatown

Dessert
egg tarts, sponge cake, mango pudding

Being Chinese…Not

As a young boy, I noticed in Chinatown there were two greetings to friends and strangers. For friends, the greeting was, "Have you eaten yet?" This saying came from the time when famine and starvation was common in China and was meant as a friendly gesture, an expression of concern. The other greeting was for strangers. For example, if you meet someone new, the first question to ask is, "What is your last name?" to be followed with, "And from what village?"

In my case, the answer to the first question was "Wong" but because there are two Chinese characters for Wong, the follow up question would be, "And which Wong?" My Wong in Chinese calligraphy is what they call a three-stroke Wong. Three evenly spaced horizontal lines with a middle vertical stroke. The meaning is Royalty. The other Wong, in Chinese calligraphy, means Yellow. Yellow as in the royal colour of the Emperor and in a sense, both Wongs pertain to the First Emperor of China.

However, growing up in Chinatown and looking at the world around me made me realize that there were disadvantages to being Chinese. For one thing, I had to go to Chinese language school after regular school. Did John go to Italian language school after school? No. I hated living in the back of the store like most other kids in Chinatown. I wished I had a house, my own bedroom, and more space. I hated being different from everyone else. As I moved into my teen years, I denied being Chinese even though Father said to me, "Look in the mirror. You're Chinese and you can't change that."

That was true, but I wanted to be Canadian. At that stage I wasn't sure what defined Canadian other than being like the lo fans. Even Jennie didn't like being Chinese. She told me that when she was little, she read in the book, *Little Women*, how a character tried to change the shape of her nose by wearing a clothespin when sleeping. Jennie also tried it, much to Father's disgust. He probably laughed quietly in private.

Many years later while visiting my sister in Edmonton, I was introduced to one of her non-Chinese friends. The friend looked at me in great astonishment and shook my hand. I was puzzled by her expression but didn't remark on it. Later in Vancouver, my sister phoned and explained by quoting her friend: "Jennie,

Three generations of Wongs. Warren, Larry, Wah, Michael, Timothy, and Nicolas in 1993

I didn't realise until I met your brother that you're Chinese!"
Wouldn't it be nice if the whole world were just as colour blind?

IDENTITY
AM I CHINESE, CANADIAN, OR CHINESE HYPHEN CANADIAN?

Father, being an immigrant from China, knew who he was to his
dying days. His identity had been forged by racial discrimination
and denial of the franchise. He paid taxes like everyone else, but he
couldn't vote. He could actually live anywhere outside Chinatown,
but he knew he was safer there. Politics and time separated him
from his first family in China, yet he continued to support them
through war and peace. He knew who he was and yet his descen-
dants have mixed feelings. Both my siblings consider themselves
Yellow Bananas, yellow on the outside and white on the inside.
As a teenager, and before I turned fifty, I also considered myself
a Yellow Banana, but I began to realize that my values were mis-
placed. For me, Father defined his identity when he sang opera
before falling asleep. The opera represented the best of times for
him because they were with Mother, he was at the peak of his
career, and life was at its best. I think that was a defining moment

Larry and Timothy

for him. I know I will never be like my father and I suppose it is not expected of me, but I am the last of his family and without sons to carry the family into the future. By putting my memories into written words Father will remain alive. If I can convey his values, his love, and his person through these words, I will have left a legacy and need not worry about carrying on the family line.

INFANT RETROSPECT

As a child brought up by a single-parent father, I was intensely curious about my mother, who had died when I was a year and a half old. I had no memory of her whatsoever. It wasn't so bad when I was growing up, but as an adult, I became obsessed by the awareness that a large part of my early life was missing. Oh certainly, I asked my siblings and father what Mother was like. They said she had been a funny and loving mother who loved me and my brothers and sister and father. She had been wonderful in the kitchen, taking time to use a small grindstone to grind rice and beans for snacks and condiments. She and Father took part in Chinese opera as players and enjoyed every minute of it. She helped Father with his business at the tailor shop. I vividly remember Chut Ghoo, her best friend. In my school years, she visited me regularly. It was only later that I found out that Father had sent me to live with her as I was too much of a handful for him when he also had to look after my two brothers and sister.

Mother's portrait that hung prominently in the living room revealed that she loved fine clothing and jewellery, but still I had no real sense of her. But one day in 1984 I visited a psychic fair where a lady offered to do a past life regression through hypnosis.

"Yes," she said, "I can hypnotize people and help regress them to their past lives."

"I'm not interested in my past lives," I said, "I want to remember my mother. She died when I was a year and a half old."

Without hesitation, she said, "I can do that."

Portrait of Mother

Three days later, I was in Anna's living room. She told me she would put me into a hypnotic trance. I'd be very relaxed and conscious of what was happening. I'd be able to choose how I wanted the session to go. She was there to guide and clarify whatever I saw. I lay down on a foam mattress in the middle of her living room floor. Next to the couch on the end table was a small tape recorder with a microphone attached to a long cable. Anna blindfolded me with a black silk handkerchief and over it put a sleeping mask. She placed the microphone on top of my chest and tested the tape recorder to make certain it worked. Then she draped a light blanket over me.

I was in a dark world, relaxed. Random images crossed my field of vision hinting at people and places. Anna spoke quietly, "Picture a clear sky and see yourself walking across a meadow. The meadow is green and lush. Ahead of you, there is a pond. Walk slowly to the edge and look into the water. Can you see your reflection?"

"Yes."

"Step into the pond. Don't be afraid of the water, just step in and walk along the bottom of the pond. As you walk forward, look upwards. Now tell me. What do you see?"

In this world, I looked up and saw the shimmering reflection of the afternoon sun. I thought, I'm looking at the sun from the bottom of a pond and yet I can breathe!

"Look into the sun, Larry," said Anna, "and let your mind pick an image for you."

The sun bathed my being with its light. It was unbelievable, but I was warm from the sun and in time I merged with the bright light. I can't remember how long I was in the light, but gradually I saw my mother's photograph. It was the studio portrait that hung in the living room. In it she is seated in a rattan chair, dressed in a high-collared silk brocade jacket and a long black silk shirt. Her legs are crossed at the ankles showing her mid-heel shoes. She looks like an elegant lady from China who did well in Canada in the thirties.

I stared at the portrait and was drinking in its details when the black and white turned to colour. Puzzled, I asked Anna why, and she said to keep looking. I felt light-headed and found myself floating above the photographer's studio where the picture was taken. Below me, I saw Mother sitting in the high back rattan chair, posing against the studio backdrop, the photographer's head under the black cloth of his tripod-mounted camera. I was in the studio of C.B. Wand, a famous Chinese photographer in Vancouver's Chinatown. Father stood in the darkness, just at the edge of the floodlights. It all felt so real. Was it my imagination or had I become a spirit? I certainly moved freely above and what was remarkable was that I could see my mother's profile and the back of her head, perspectives not seen in a photograph.

As if I was dreaming, the reality shifted and I was transported to China and its craggy mountains and hills. I was flying above a river and following a man sailing a sampan towards the dock at a small village. I flew over the village and saw a busy street filled people, horses, and carts. Not far away was a red temple or pavilion. I saw two women approaching a house. Inside the front room was a picture of Mother.

Although the women were talking, I couldn't hear what they were saying, but it appeared they were paying their respects to Mother. I had the impression that this was her village and family house. I was then surrounded by red colour. There were no patterns or shapes, yet I had the sensation of being pulled back until the distinct texture of brocade came into focus. I looked down and saw that I was wearing a Chinese opera costume. Anna asked me to say what I was wearing on my feet. I looked and spread my arms. My sleeves were long and wide, the brocade ended halfway up my forearm, and a white linen cuff extended to my wrist. I was wearing wooden sandals on two short stilts. I felt briefly that I was my mother. The next thing I knew, I was at the back of the crowded theatre, and there on stage was Mother with the same costume and wearing heavy make-up. She strutted across the stage, relishing the part of the General, resplendent in the footlights. Superimposed on this was her photograph. I suppose it confirmed that the vision was indeed Mother. She was one of the few women in the early Chinese Republic to act on stage. Prior to 1911, no Chinese women had been allowed to be actresses.

Blackness crept into my vision. I complained to Anna, who assured me I would see something and that I should just relax. Then, an image formed and the darkness fell away. I saw Mother's face over me. I was on my back. She rubbed noses with me and laughed. I smiled and realized I was a baby in her arms. Her face was slightly distorted, probably due to my baby's eyes. In the next instant I was in spirit form floating above the living quarters at the back of Father's tailor shop. I saw my sister Jennie, aged eight, and my teenaged brothers.

I was a baby and Mother was feeding me with a bottle of milk. My sister and brothers were waiting for their turns to feed me. Father looked on smiling. Mother burped me and returned me to the crib. I closed my eyes and felt the warmth of the bed. In the darkness of my closed eyes, I saw Mother's photograph gradually replaced by one of the whole family.

As I stared at the photograph, I found myself floating in the photographer's studio. The photographer carefully adjusted his camera, signalled he was ready, and ducked under a black cloth. The family smiled happily and when they heard the click of the shutter, they walked away. Darkness fell and I waited for what seemed to be a long time. Black as ink. I felt like I was suspended and looking directly below me. Pitch dark gave way to dimness.

Mother was lying on the bed. There were shadows around her from a bed lamp. She was wearing a blouse and a blanket covered the rest of her. She was coughing in pain. I knew she was dying. I told Anna my mother was alone, but Anna said to look again. In the gloom, I could see Father's hand holding hers. Mother stopped coughing. I waited. Suddenly I felt myself being pulled away until I was in darkness. It was as if my back was attached to a spear and someone was lifting it up. I was moving towards a bright light and as I got closer, I saw Mother, and angelic figures of people she had known. Was I experiencing Mother's journey to the other side? Darkness fell like a curtain.

I saw Mother once again in bed, and by her side, Father was crying. My throat caught and tears welled in my eyes. My spirit shrank and I was drawn in Father's direction and entered his body. His grief became mine and I cried in front of Anna. It had taken 45 years but I finally cried over my Mother's death. Although I had such a brief experience of her, because I touched her and felt her person, I knew she was a real person from my past.

I next saw Father, but sensed I was to witness his death as well. Memories of his death seeped into my vision. He had died eighteen years previously. I told Anna I didn't want to go through it again but she assured me I would feel no pain or emotions and that I would just be an observer. I went back to the exact moment of Father's death. He had been in the intensive care unit at the hospital. Tubes were in his nose and arms. His eyes were closed. When he stopped breathing the whole scene froze. I felt weightless again, and in spirit form, I was pushed away from him upwards into the darkness to a shining light until I saw him with Mother in the afterlife.

I smiled when he joined Mother. After her death, he had not remarried. His love for her had carried on. Mother saw me and walked over to embrace me. Together we walked across a misty field, and overhead, the sky turned a vivid blue. I saw a vase with pink and red roses. Mother embraced me again and my vision was awash in pink.

My session ended when Anna took me to the present and gradually drew me from my trance. My body was cold and my joints were sore. The sleeping mask and black silk handkerchief along with the microphone were removed. The subdued light was hard on my eyes and I was awash in fatigue and numbness. An hour and a half had gone by. Anna gave me a welcome cup of hot tea when I sat up. My mind was filled with amazement: my thoughts leaped about wildly. I saw what I had come for.

CLOSING THE CIRCLE

I am weary from jet lag but blink to keep awake. My flight was long and late. It is midnight Hong Kong time, fifteen hours ahead of my Vancouver clock. My body is confused. No matter. I am in a cocktail lounge with my nephew, his wife, and their teenage daughter. We are on the Kowloon side and sitting in a comfortable leather booth sipping our drinks. We face the floor to ceiling windows and admire the lights of the Hong Kong towers with their reflections glistening in the waters of Victoria Harbour. My nephew, Gum Yuen, nudges me and points. "See that?" he says. "That was where the handover ceremony took place three years ago." The Convention Centre sits on the waterfront and looks like a matchbox against a forest of towering glass and concrete. I recognize the landmark Bank of China tower with its laced up girdle.

"Are you happy Hong Kong is back in China's hands?" I ask.

"Of course. Hong Kong's return to China was the best thing to ever happen. It's like coming back to family." Lucy, his wife, nods in agreement. He sips his drink. "There were doubts as to what would happen after the handover but the changes aren't too bad. It's good that Hong Kong is back in China's hands."

I had been to Hong Kong before as a tourist, but this trip was personal. For the last year or so, I had wanted to find my relatives in China. Father, who came to Canada in 1911, had left a wife and son behind. He was what we call in Cantonese a wah kiu, an overseas Chinese. Like most Chinese of his generation, he had left home to make his fortune in Canada. He must have done well because ten years later, he sent for my mother, paid her $500 head tax, and married her almost as soon as she got off the boat. Father lived in a time when first marriages were often arranged, and if a man could afford it, he would take on additional wives. Now here I am in Hong Kong, to meet the children of my eldest half brother. I never met him. He died more than ten years ago. We were separated not only by a different mother and an ocean but also by a generation and dissimilar societies.

Debbie sips her soft drink and asks, "Mum told me you found us on the Internet. How did you do that?"

"I did a Google search and found a bulletin board called Chinese Surnames Queries. It was mostly about genealogy, but there were questions about where to find relatives and home villages. I decided to give it a try and wrote that I was looking for my father's village, called Lung Tow Wan."

"Cool."

"It took six months before I got a reply. We exchanged emails and I found out that Bert is an architect from Los Angeles working in Singapore. He said he could help find my village because his grandfather was from there. Also Bert had been to the village several times. One day, he told me his Hong Kong cousin was going to visit the village and asked if I had any photographs of my father and family. I emailed him what he requested and a couple of weeks later, he said his cousin had found your parents."

Lucy says, "That's right. Our respective cousins worked together in the same commune. I gave his cousin my phone number for you to call us."

My nephew raises his glass in a toast, "And here we are. Welcome to Hong Kong. Tomorrow we'll take you to the village."

The next day, my nephew and Lucy pick me up in his BMW at my hotel near Nathan Road and we drive to the China Ferry Terminal. We arrive early, go to the departure level with our tickets, and then through immigration, and then finally to the waiting lounge. It is the first of May, the Labour Day week for the Chinese, which explains why there are few people around when we board a catamaran appropriately named *Zhongshan*, after the county capital near my father's village.

Zhongshan pushes gently away from the dock and points its bow into the estuary. The catamaran is a sleek-looking vessel, streamlined for speed and powered by twin engines. Once it clears the inner harbour, it accelerates to cruising speed, leaving a V-shaped wake. We speed past freighters, scows, riverboats, and other ferries under a bright blue sky. A hostess with a trolley comes by offering hot tea which we gladly accept as we pull down the small table from the back of the seat in front. Outside the window, the flat emerald land stretches endlessly to the distant mountains.

I shiver with excitement. This is the land of my father. This is the way he came to Canada. Did he experience the same thrill of leaving his home as I am feeling coming to his home? I lean back in my seat and turn to Lucy.

"When I get to the village, I'd like to visit my brother's grave." She looks at me with interest.

"Before I left Vancouver, I visited my father's grave and told him I would visit the home village."

"That's good," she says. "You're showing your respect for your ancestors."

"Do you believe in spirits?" I ask.

I answer before she can.

"My father died in January of 1966. That was in Vancouver. Four years later, I was promoted and posted to Ottawa and Toronto. The first winter I spent there, I dreamt of Father. When I woke up one particular day, I noticed the date. It was the same date as my father's death. The next year, I had the same dream and on the same date. I couldn't understand it. I hadn't thought of the date before sleeping and certainly I never thought of my father. These dreams kept up on the same date until I moved back to Vancouver ten years later. But that year in January, the dream didn't return and never did again."

Lucy nods and says, "It sounds like your father was looking after you when you were away from home and when you came back, he felt it was no longer necessary." I tell her I have brought some soil from Father's grave that I want to mix in with Yung Tai's grave. Lucy says she remembers my half brother as a very good man. Like my grandfather, he was a chef. Even Yuen is a good cook, better than her, she laughs. The more we talk, the more we seemed to have in common. I tell her my eldest brother was training to be a chef. And my father was a good cook, too. I also learned to cook for myself.

We reach the Zhongshan port an hour and a half later. Going through immigration is a perfunctory experience and outside the building, a driver from my nephew's factory is waiting for us. We pile into the Toyota mini-bus and drive through the flat and featureless countryside. Our first stop is the factory, located in an industrial park setting. It is neither small nor large. It reminds me of a giant cube three stories high with a glass-tiled corner.

My great-nephew takes me to where men work on silk-screens as wide layers of blank cloth roll from a giant drum past them. At the other end, the finished painted cloths hang on dry-ing racks suspended from the ceiling. The new prints are floral designs for bedsheets. There are also cartoon figures for children's clothing. I give my nephew a thumbs-up. "You know," he says, "twenty years ago, I was desperate to move to Canada, but I couldn't get a sponsor. Now I'm glad I stayed. China is prospering and you know something else? I have friends who owned their businesses in China, then migrated to Canada only to work as pizza delivery boys. Can you imagine that? A pizza delivery boy! What a letdown."

We climb into another car with Gum Yuen's business partner at the wheel and head to Sekki, otherwise known as Zhongshan city, the county capital. Industrial buildings greet us on the city's edge. As we approach the centre, high-rises, including the Zhongshan International Hotel and its revolving restaurant on top, come into view. Lucy explains that the main street was once a two-lane street, but that it has been widened to three-lanes. At one intersection, pedestrian walkways arch over the busy street corners to allow for the smooth flow of traffic. As it is Labour Day, most businesses are closed and few people are on the streets, but it takes a while before we reach the end of town. I hold my breath. We are nearing Father's village.

As long as I can remember, I have stared at a postcard of Lung Tow Wan, the village. The postcard showed a group of block-like buildings, no more than two or three stories high, with tiled roofs. Among the buildings was a tall tower. It was cylindri-cal in shape and topped off by a cupola. There was also a narrow river that flowed from the horizon, turned just behind the tower, and went the length of the village.

I asked Father about the tall tower. "What is it?"

"A gun tower."

"A gun tower? Why?"

"In the early days bandits and warlords raided our village. The tower was manned by guards who gave warning of any raids and shot down marauders."

We turn left onto a narrow road with trees on both sides. Ahead was a familiar sight. I recognize the landmarks from the postcard. There's the bend in the river but where is the tower? As if to answer my silent question, my nephew points to a flat white concrete foundation. "That was where the gun tower was." The small river becomes a canal. We drive along a narrow street, past homes in compounds, not a space between them, no lawns and no trees. The concrete buildings with their orange-tiled roofs stand mute, almost at attention, ready for inspection. We cross a little bridge and stop in front of a three-storey building. "Here it is," says Lucy. "Your father's home."

The house is three-stories, and its property defined by a low wall like a European villa. It looks new. "The original building was torn down," says Lucy. "And this was built in place of it. Come on in, your nephews and nieces are waiting for you." We enter the yard and go through the front door. The living room is full of people, my father's grandchildren and their children. At once they start to chatter while my nephew and Lucy introduce me. The family resemblance is startling, particularly in facial features such as the shape of eyebrows, the broad forehead, and the flat nose. We are tied together by my father's blood. One glance at them gives away our common ancestor, my father, their grandfather.

They all seem to know about my life up to a certain point because when Father was alive, he not only sent money to support his family, he kept in touch with First Wife at least once a month, telling her about the family in Vancouver. He kept writing except for a period during the Sino-Japanese War and World War Two. When the Communists took the country in 1949 from the Nationalists, Father was worried when no letters from him were acknowledged. Finally he received a letter from Hong Kong. The letter was not from First Wife but from an administrator who assured Father that his family was safe and that he should con-

Pop's home village, Lung Tow Wan in the early 1900s

tinue to send money, but perhaps with a little more than usual to guarantee their safety. Father swore and called it blackmail. He had no choice however but to give in. He had read newspaper reports about the terrible turmoil in China and he, along with his compatriots, was helpless to do anything about it. The instruction from Hong Kong was to mail the money to a post office box and not to the village. Within a year, he heard from First Wife, who mailed a photograph of the family with other relatives in front of a train station. The group wore clean clothes and all smiled into the camera. Life under Communist rule was good.

I shake hands with all those in the room. Lucy takes my arm and we walk through the house. She shows me the kitchen, a den, and a storeroom. Upstairs are the bedrooms. Despite the hot weather outside, it is cool inside the house. We step out onto one of the bedroom balconies overlooking the waterway. The air is hot and I am perspiring. At one time, I could bear the heat but now that I'm over sixty, it's not possible any more.

Larry at centre with first family in China

Lucy points to a narrow, three-storey building with a large banyan tree in front. "That's your brother's house. He thought it was good to have his family there, close to the main house." I smile and shake my head in wonder. It is possible to see over the top of the village. There are no high-rises or tall buildings. Probably the tallest is only four stories. To my left is a rice field. I gasp. I can't believe it. In astonishment, I say to Lucy, "When I was young, my father told me why he left the village. He said that there was famine in the land that the river was drying up, that there were no fish, and that the rice field was drying up." I pause. "I thought he telling me a tall tale but it looks like it was true." Lucy smiles. "You must feel as though you are seeing through his eyes."

My brother's house is cool. In the living room on a mantel, I see a photograph of my brother as an old man; next to it is a portrait of my father as a young man, with a crew cut and western style shirt, tie, and jacket, sitting in a chair. This discovery is even more exciting because there is a young ten-year-old First Son standing on Father's right and, on the other side, his two wives. The two women, dressed in traditional Chinese gowns, sit demurely side by side. I vaguely remember my father telling me stories of his First Wife and Son but to see the photograph of them together is reality hitting me in the face like cold water.

In the afternoon, my nephew takes me on a tour of the village. He shows me where Father attended school, the grotto where he drew fresh water, and the streets where he must have walked. Occasionally a lone rider on a motor scooter buzzes by, then the streets are quiet once again.

Later, with Lisa, a niece and the youngest of the clan, we

Larry and nephew in front of the plaque thanking Larry's nephew's donation to the home village's school

drive to the cemetery on the outskirts of the village. We chat in English and I find out that she is in her last year at the local university. After I return home, we keep in touch by email.

The ancient cemetery is crowded with mausoleums. We find my brother's gravesite, which is circular with a raised crescent-shaped terrace. The names of my brother, his wife, and Father's First Wife are engraved on a plaque in the centre of the crescent. I bow three times as Lisa looks on. From my pocket, I pull out the vial, go down on my right knee and carefully tap the soil to spread below the headstone. It is symbolic. I want to bring my father back to his village, back to his son, and back to First Wife. His last visit to the village was in 1929: he lived for another thirty-seven years, and never saw his family in China again.

I put my hand on the headstone, and like a needle on a phonograph record, run my index finger from left to right on the raised calligraphy of the three names. I hear Father's voice telling me why he left the village. He must have yearned for the voice and touch of his son, and for First Wife, he must have ached for her warmth and smiles. Those must have been lonely years for him. I imagine that Father would have thought about what might have happened if he had been there to see his son through the growing-up years.

I breathe a sigh and feel release. My father is back where he wanted to be. I know he loved my mother but it seems to me, the first love, whether arranged or not, remains forever in memory, never to be forgotten, but to be cherished as long as one lives. A shiver runs through me. I reach out for Lisa to help me up and as she does so, the distance between generations and cultures blurs, and for a moment, we are truly family.

Father working in the kitchen

photo credit Albert Tsui

Larry Wong was born in Vancouver's Chinatown in 1938 and attended Strathcona School and Vancouver Tech High School. After attending the University of British Columbia in the late fifties, he began a career with the federal government, retiring in 1994. Since then he has been active in various community activities such as the Chinese Canadian Historical Society of British Columbia, Tamahnous Theatre, Federation of BC Writers, and Chinese Canadian Military Museum. He has written in newspapers and magazines and currently writes in a blog, Ask Larry, at www.cchsbc.ca. He loves to spend time in Hawaii.